Walks
Snowdonia
Mountains

Don Hinson

First edition: March 1987
Revised edition: 1997
Revised edition: 2009

ISBN: 978-1-84524-092-9

First published in 1989 by Gwasg Carreg Gwalch

Revised edition published in 2009 by Llygad Gwalch,
Ysgubor Plas, Llwyndyrys, Pwllheli, Gwynedd LL53 6NG
01758 750432 01758 750438
books@carreg-gwalch.com
Web site: www.carreg-gwalch.com

ABOUT THE AUTHOR

Don Hinson was a physics teacher whose chief relaxation was, and still is, walking in the country with his wife. He drew the maps and sketches for this book and she did the typing. He has also written books on physics, *Handbook of Chiltern Hill Walks, Discovering Walks in Lakeland Mountains, New Walks in Snowdonia and Walks in North Snowdonia.*

CONTENTS

One of the falls on Afon Llafar seen on walk 3A.

LIST OF WALKS

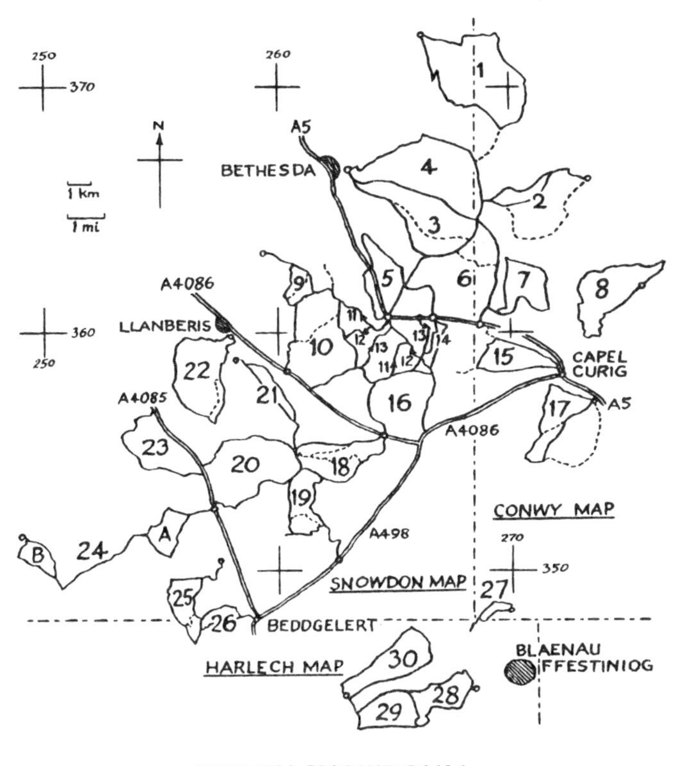

NORTH SNOWDONIA

Note: (a) many of the walks can be shortened or extended; (b) the last figure in brackets is the total height climbed. (1ft is 0.3048m.)

* An asterisk indicates that the walk has an alternative route which is often shorter.

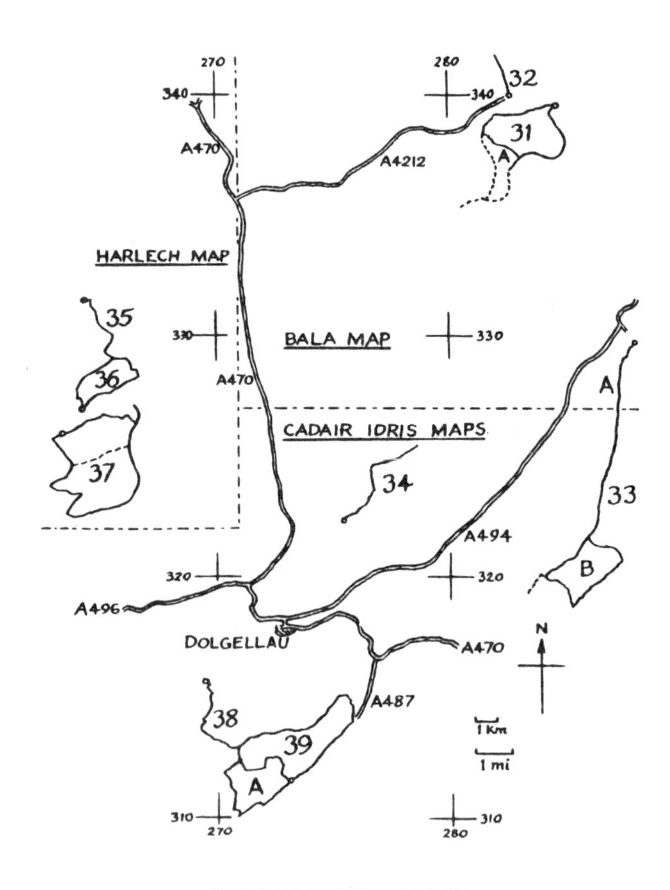

SOUTH SNOWDONIA

Hazards and Problems
Take notice, take care

The author and the publishers stress that walkers should be aware of the dangers that may occur on all walks.

- check local weather forecast before walking; do not walk up into mist or low clouds
- use local OS maps side by side with walking guides
- wear walking boots and clothing
- do not take any unnecessary risks – conditions can change suddenly and can vary from season to season
- take special care when accompanied by children or dogs
- when walking on roads, ensure that you are conspicuous to traffic from either direction

Please note that the terms 'easier', 'easy' are only used in this book in comparison to the most dangerous and challenging routes to the summits of Snowdonia.

INTRODUCTION

This book describes 45 walks, mostly circular, varying in length from 3.5 km (2¼ miles) to 16 km (10 miles). Some of its special points are:

- All Snowdonian mountains over 2250 feet high are included, and some lower ones.
- Routes are chosen to reveal the natural beauty of the mountains with the minimum of difficult, tedious or unpleasant sections.
- The written route description is always beside the relevant map — not on another page.
- Route numbers on both map and written description make it easy to relate one to the other.
- The maps are accurately drawn and easily related to Ordnance Survey maps.

Snowdonia is a splendid and wild area of North Wales, noted for its rugged mountains, remote upland lakes and pools, from which tumble rocky streams and waterfalls, and its natural woods and plantations clothing the lower slopes and valleys. For more details pay a visit to your library — this book concentrates on the walking to keep its price down.

There are a variety of mountain ranges and areas to choose from, each with its own special characteristics:

(1) The Carneddau (walks 1 to 8) occupy a vast area N of the A5 stretching nearly to the coast and the Conwy Valley. From Llyn Ogwen a magnificent high ridge runs NE keeping continuously above 2900 ft for 10 km (6 mi). Many side ridges make a wide choice of walks possible, though most of them are fairly long.

(2) The Glyderau (walks 9 to 16) are a more compact range between the A5 and A4086 (Llanberis Pass) roads. The main ridge starts near the slate quarries S of Bethesda and ends at Capel Curig. There are many splendid ways up to the ridge, mainly from the A5, giving a good choice of walks of reasonable length. The section near Llyn Ogwen has the finest rock scenery and some attractive mountain lakes. Most routes have some steep and rough sections.

(3) Moel Siabod (walk 17) is somewhat isolated but should not be neglected. It has fine rocky ridges and lakes.
(4) The Snowdon area (walks 18 to 22) is well known and the paths well defined. The superb views can be enjoyed using routes chosen to be easy or tough according to your needs. Nearby Moel Eilio offers an easy circuit not far NW of Snowdon.
(5) The Nantlle area (walks 23 to 26) contains two ridges — the excellent Nantlle ridge and the lesser known but worthwhile Moel Hebog ridge. To the N Mynydd Mawr provides a fine outing that is less strenuous.
(6) The Moelwyn area (walks 27 to 30) abounds with old quarries which add interest to these generally easier and shorter walks. Highlights are the rocky Cnicht ridge and the equally rocky section between Moelwyn Bach and Mawr.
(7) The Arenig area (walks 31 and 32) stands in isolation to the E. Arenig Fawr has a fine lake and rocky summit and ridge.
(8) The Aran ridge (walk 33) runs S from near Bala. The ridge is attractive, but access to it is limited.
(9) Rhobell Fawr (walk 34) has an easy non-circular walk in a pleasant area where few walkers are likely to be met.
(10) The Rhinogydd (walks 35 to 37) are part of a remote ridge built on different and older rocks (Cambrian) compared with those of the north. The ridge is wildest and roughest at the N end, but mostly grassy and less exciting S of Y Llethr. A drive along miles of narrow roads is needed to reach starting points. Often the paths are not well defined.
(11) Cadair Idris (walks 38 and 39) makes a magnificent southern end to the National Park, with fine rocky ridges that plunge down to remote mountain lakes.

How to follow a route. A map to a scale of at least 1 inch to the mile and a compass should be taken on walks. Before using this book get to know the words used in the walks descriptions. (See glossary below.) Note that 'up' and 'down' refer to gradients (unlike everyday speech when we go down a level road). Read the walk summary when choosing a walk to see if it is likely to suit your tastes and the weather. Make sure you know the quickest way back if you have to abandon the walk at any point. Allow ample time for the walk until you get to know your capabilities. If new to mountains try some easier walks first:

9A Elidir Fach (6½ km, 4 mi, 1500 ft if E. Fawr is not visited)
18A omitting Snowdon by turning R along the 'upper path' on reaching point C (9 km, 5¾ mi, 1400 ft).
21 Snowdon (10 km, 6¼ mi, 1800 ft if you omit Snowdon by turning back at point 5).
22 Moel Eilio (11.5 km, 7¼ mi, 2400 ft).
27 Allt Fawr (5 km, 3 mi, 1100 ft).
38 Cadair Idris (9 km, 5½ mi, 2400 ft).

GLOSSARY:

Arete: narrow rocky ridge.
Cairn: heap of stones 0.5 m or more in height to mark paths, their junctions and viewpoints.
Col: the saddle shaped top of a pass.
Cwm: upper end of a valley enclosed by steep ground on three sides.
Drive: track to house or farm.
Farmgate: one wide enough for vehicles.
Lane: small surfaced road.
Leat: artificial watercourse that contours round the side of a hill.
On: keep walking in about the same direction.
Outcrop: mass of rock jutting from the ground.
Path: a way too small for vehicles.
Scramble: a steep rocky section where hands are needed as well as feet.
Scree: lots of small rocks a few inches across.
Stile: any device for crossing wall, fence or hedge.
Track: a way wide enough for vehicles.

ABBREVIATIONS

E,N,S,W: east, north, south, west.
Km, mi: Kilometre, mile.
L: left. 'Turn L' means turn about 90°; 'half L' 45°; 'one third L' 30°; 'two-thirds L' 60°; 'sharp L' 135°. 'Fork L' means take the left hand of 2 paths at a junction.
m: metre (roughly a yard)

P: parking off road. Free unless otherwise stated.
R: right
●: marks a place where there is a choice of routes.

HAZARDS AND PROBLEMS

1. Boggy patches. Wet areas have been avoided where possible, but some patches may be met. I can't promise that ones mentioned in a walk will be the only ones you find — conditions vary from year to year.
2. Snow and ice. These walks are mainly for the summer. Don't attempt them in winter conditions.
3. Strong winds. Avoid aretes like Crib Goch if windy. It usually gets windier as you gain height.
4. Mist. Do not walk up into a mist or low clouds. If rain is forecast this may also obscure the view. If caught by mist turn back if you have not reached the highest peak of the walk (unless otherwise stated). As a rule this is not difficult, but sometimes it is essential to have compass, map, warm clothing and extra food. So always take them. In the less popular walking areas it is a good idea to (1) tell someone your precise route and when you expect to get back; (2) let them know when you are safely down.
5. Rough paths. Wear walking boots with thick soles and ankle protection to make walking comfortable and safe. Scrambles in these walks are quite short and easy unless otherwise stated.

MAPS

All walks are on the excellent 1¼ inch to the mile Ordnance Survey Landranger Maps 115 (Snowdon) and 124 (Dolgellau). Walks 1 to 27 are on map 115, walks 31 to 39 on map 124; the others fall on both maps.

The 2½ inch to the mile Outdoor Leisure Maps are optional alternatives to the essential 1¼ inch maps. One of their advantages is that they show walls and fences. But be wary of paths marked in green as some of them are simply not there. (If the green is printed on top of black dashes the path is much more likely to exist).

Maps needed for each walk are listed after the title of the walk. Letter refer to the Outdoor Leisure Maps: B = Bala; CI = Cadair Idris; CV = Conwy Valley; H = Harlech; S = Snowdon.

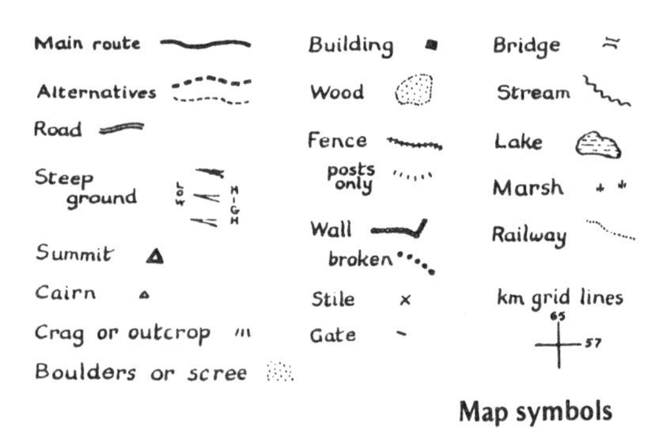

Map symbols

Note that the maps in this book show details useful for following the route described, but unnecessary detais (e.g. stiles and walls met on an obviously clear path) may not be drawn in.

Grid references are given for the starting points of the walks. The first 3 numbers refer to the grid lines showing how far East the point is; the last 3 numbers to how far North. Thus on walk 1, 663 means the start is three tenths of the way from the vertical line 66 to line 67, and 720 means the start is on line 72.

Buses run by the start of many of the walks, at least in the summer. Check the timetable before attempting to use them. Note particularly the summer Sherpa buses that give access to many walks in N Snowdonia, including Snowdon, the Glyderau and Carneddau etc.

PUBLIC ACCESS

It is not easy to decide what routes can be used by the public. Only a few are legal rights-of-way. In some areas you are free to walk anywhere e.g. in most parts of National Trust areas and Forestry Commission land. In many cases it has been a tradition that walkers have been allowed to use routes though they have no legal right to walk them. There is no official list of such routes, though a few 'courtesy' paths have been arranged with the agreement of the landowner. I hope that all my routes fall into these categories, but cannot be certain of this. I have never met anyone who has objected to my presence on a path, and most owners will accept those who respect the land and do not damage walls, let dogs chase sheep etc. Stiles over walls or fences are frequently found and are a good sign that the public is allowed there. Areas where the walking is strictly limited include the Aran and Nantlle ridges.

HOW THE ROUTES WERE CHOSEN

After a number of holidays in Snowdonia I found it was hard to devise a good day out in the mountains, because of the lack of guide books with accurate maps and full descriptions of circular walks, except for the most popular areas like Snowdon. Often it was not clear whether there was a path to follow, so to be on the safe side a return was made along the same route.

On moving into the area, I decided to write a guide to help walkers choose a walk suitable to their requirements so that their day out is more likely to be rewarding. I have made about 100 visits to the mountains over a period of 4 years, and have visited most of the available routes. After weeding out boggy or featureless routes I have tried to link the scenic, fairly dry and scree-free routes into circular walks of reasonable lengths. If a mountain has several good routes, more than one walk is described.

I am grateful for information and advice from Gwynedd County Council and the Snowdonia National Park Office which has been useful in dealing with some of the lesser known routes. Also to my wife for typing the manuscript, and to Mr D. Salter for useful comments on the routes.

1 FOEL-FRAS FROM ABER

(16 km, 10 mi, 3100 ft) Map 115, CV, S

Summary. After a lovely walk to the splendid Aber Falls the walk climbs (pathless) to a broad ridge running SE to Foel-fras. Then a descent to Drum and an easy track gets you back with good views of the sea. Adventurous walkers may like to end this walk along the Foel-ganol ridge from 699 710 to 681 714. The final descent to point 13 is steep and rough.

Park near road bridge (663 720) 1 km (¾ mi) SE from the road junction on the A55 at Aber.

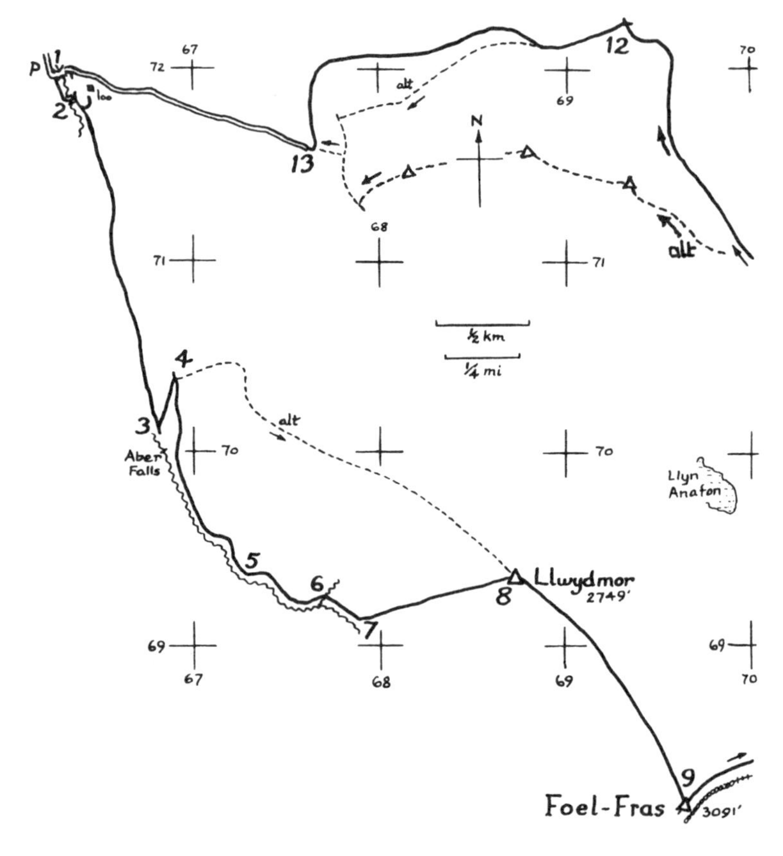

1 At road bridge take the footpath by the river, which is on your left until you cross a footbridge. **2** Here bear R up the valley track. (Ignore the sharp U-turn on your L.) **3** Go sharp L up path when about 100 m from the waterfall. **4** At the forest there is a choice of routes. The easiest follows the edge of the forest until the corner where you go SE up the ridge (no path) to Llwydmor, and follow 8. The best way is sharp right along a gently rising path. This crosses scree and bare ground (where path rather awkwardly tilts sideways) before becoming an enjoyable high level route above the falls. **5** Path becomes vague for a short distance about 100 m beyond some stone enclosures. Keep fairly near stream until path is clearer again and then bears away from stream to avoid a rushy area. **6** Cross a side stream near a waterfall on the main one. The path is soon about 50 m L of main stream. **7** At cairn on bouldery patch 100 m before a good waterfall go half L up grass towards rocky outcrop on skyline.

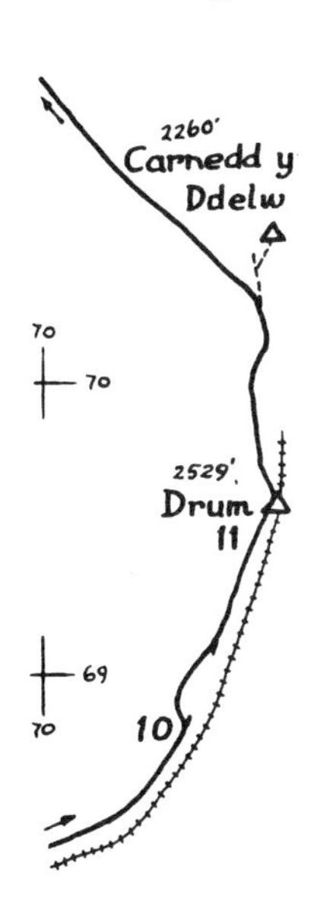

(No path. You walk on grass and a few small patches of boulders and low shrubs.) Keep on past this outcrop to the big cairn on the bouldery top of Llwydmor. **8** Go SE down the broad ridge and up to Foel-fras. (No path, but easy grass. Patches of scree can be dodged.) **9** Here go L near wall, then fence (on your R) along path. **10** At bottom of slope fork L along smaller path which soon bears R towards Drum. (The larger path may be wetter.) **11** At Drum go N on clear track. (After it turns half L a small path by a cairn can be used to make short detour to Carnedd y Ddelw. After 100 m leave this path and go up easy grass to the huge summit cairn). **12** Go L at cross-tracks. Follow the track to the lane. (Or if you want a change from the stony track go on the level grass path 100 m after the track bears half R. It is vague in places, but a line of rushes is a clue to where it goes. It gently descends to a track. Go L along track and soon sharp R to lane). **13** Down lane to start.

2 THE CARNEDDAU FROM THE EAST

(14 km, 8¾ mi, 2300 ft) Map 115, CV,S.)

1 Go R (NW) through gate and along track. **2** Cross bridge at Melynllyn and take the path that goes roughly W up a grassy ridge between two lakes. When path fades keep going straight up the slope finally W to ridge top. **3** Go W to join ridge path, where good views down the other side can be seen. There go L along ridge path to Carnedd Llywelyn (or R to Foel grach. To the R you can go 3 km (2 mi) without dropping below 2900 ft). Return the same way to 3. **4** Now go roughly SE down towards the ridge

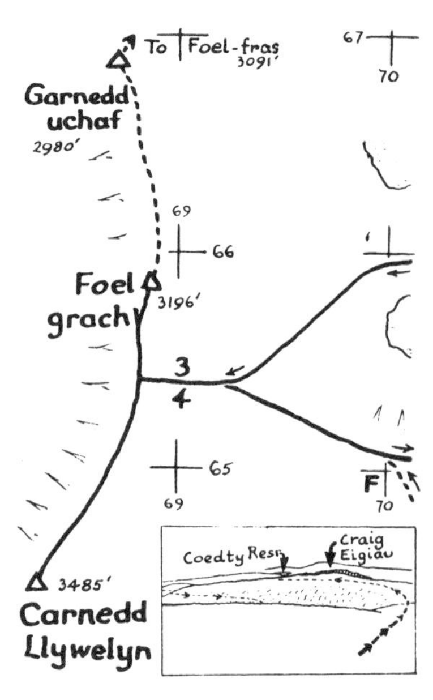

on the R of Melynllyn (see drawing). There is no path until nearly down the gentle slope. There follow the path E/NE across the broad ridge with steep ground not far to your L. **5** When near the rocky top of Craig Eigiau it is worth leaving the path to visit it. Then bear L (N) to rejoin the path where a fence is met (on your R). **6** Follow the fence along the ridge top. **7** Follow the wall (on your R) which bears L of the ridge top. (Or stay on the ridge using faint path which may have a few wet patches. Later go down dry grass (no path) by wall on your R to join the track you started along). **8** Soon you join the track you started along, and go on down it back to the start.

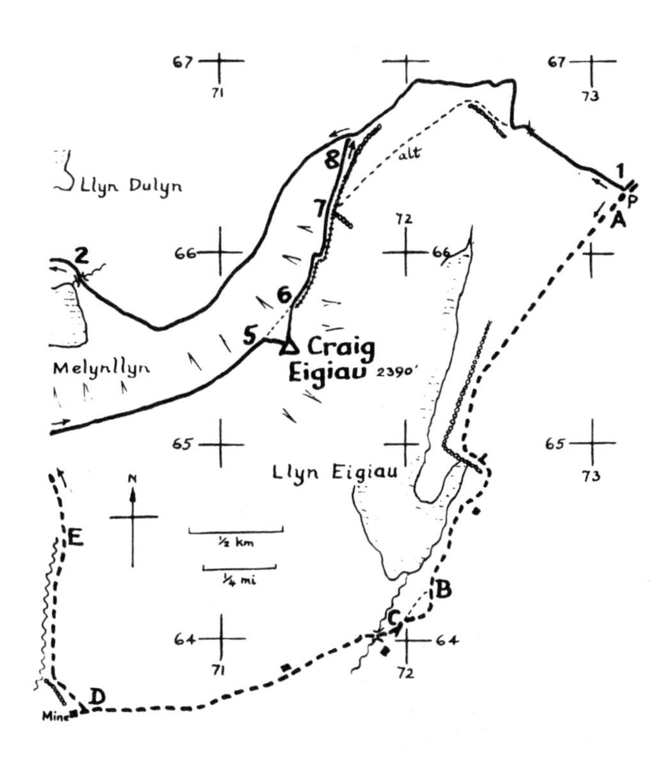

2A Alternative ascent (16 km, 10 mi, 2300 ft)
A Go on (SW) along track which later runs beside Llyn Eigiau. **B** Near the end of the lake the track rises and soon falls again. (There is a level short cut which can be wet.) **C** 100 m before building, fork half R to bridge and go on to mine. **D** Just at the first mine ruins go half R along path. It crosses a marshy area and then climbs beside a sunken stream (on your L) mainly on dry grass, but with some boggy patches. **E** When path fades go on up gentle slope to ridge path. **F** Go up this path, and keep on (roughly NW) when this also fades. At ridge top follow stage 3 of the main walk.

Summary. The start is reached by a rough and narrow mountain road best avoided at weekends and in the main holiday season. A good track leads to a small lake. The main ridge is reached after a further mile. Here Carnedd Llywelyn may be visited. For a shorter walk go to Foel grach instead, saving you 1½ km (1 mi). The return is down a pleasant ridge with the choice of visiting, with little effort, the attractive rocky top of the crags that rise behind Llyn Eigiau. It is a fairly long walk but quite easy as you start at 1200 feet, and the gradients are gentle. The alternative ascent is longer and wetter and a wall stops you seeing Llyn Eigiau at first.

Because there are pathless sections do not go beyond points 2 or D when there is a mist. If there is mist at 4 follow the instructions, and if in doubt bear L so that you keep along the edge of the flat area with the slope down to Melynllyn just on your L.

Park at the end (732 663) of the road that climbs from Tal-y-bont (767 688) in the Conwy Valley.

Ysgolion Duon (Black Ladders) as seen on walk 3.

3 THE CARNEDDAU FROM GERLAN

(14 km, 8¾ mi, 3400 ft) Map 115, S, (CV)

Summary. After an attractive start along a lane some wet patches may be crossed before a good ridge is climbed to Carnedd Dafydd. Then follows a superb 5 km (3 mi) of ridge keeping at 3000 ft or more. After the first short steep descent from Yr Elen the return down the ridge is quite easy. The alternative valley ascent is harder to follow. It leaves out Carnedd Dafydd and half the ridge, but impressive crags are seen. If mist comes down on the high ridge, the path and terrain make it possible to carry on to Carnedd Llywelyn where a compass should ensure you descend the correct ridge.

Parking. If on the A5 going N, take the first R turn (627 660) at the outskirts of Bethesda. Sharp R at crossroads. Park in the second turning on L, 'Stryd Morgan Street' (632 664), or nearby.

1 At the bottom of Stryd Morgan turn L (SE) along road. **2** After first bridge bear R at road junction to next bridge. Here road bears L to stile 50m beyond bridge. **3** Over stile and on along L edge of field. Go L over stile just before ruin and then R 50 m to gap. **4** Go L of second ruin to cross 2 streams 30 m to its L and follow grass path by wall (on your R) to a ravine. Then turn R to a wall gap. **5** Here go one third R for 30 m along faint path and one third L along a path towards a tree. It becomes clearer and drier as you proceed. **6** After a wet patch go over stile 30 m R of wall gap.

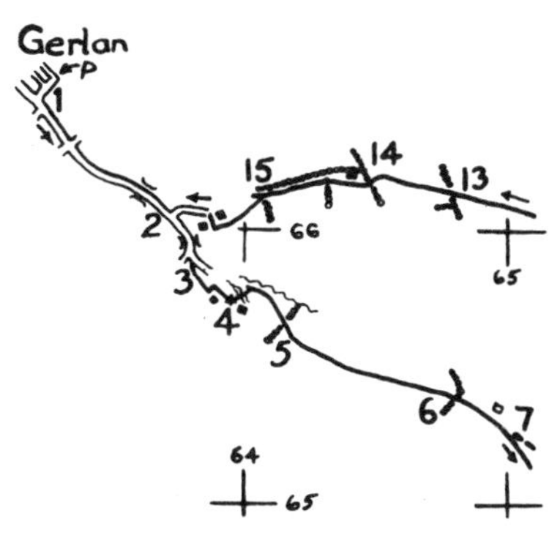

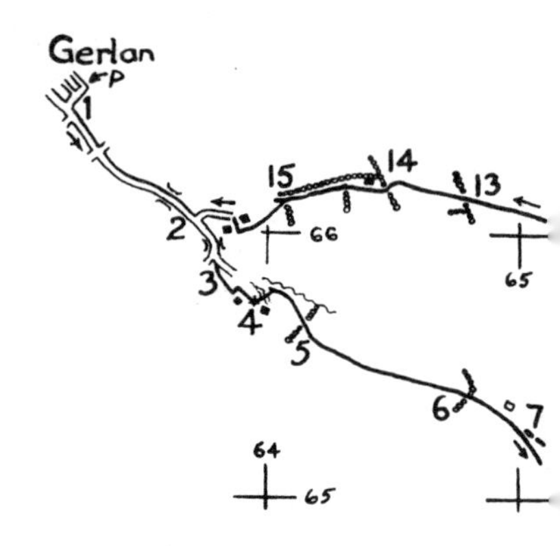

7 Soon after passing an enclosure on the L leave the path and turn half R up the ridge. Later keep near steep ground on your L for good views of crags, etc. **8** At a slaty top with cairn go on gently down, still with steep ground on your L. Then bear L straight up stony ground to Carnedd Dafydd. **9** Follow path L (E) to Carnedd Llywelyn, with steep ground on your L most of the way and also on your R before the final climb. (Keep nearer the edge than the path does to enjoy the views.) **10** Here turn L (W) to low jagged outcrops and find the cairned path going NW towards the crags of Yr Elen. It keeps just R of a large bouldery area and then goes down grass and up to the summit with crags on your R. **11** A cairn marks the top of the steep winding path NW down the ridge. Keep on down the ridge (with a path sometimes) passing just L of outcrops and scree patches. **12** After the last steepish descent keep on W/NW towards a wall/fence T-junction with a shed well behind it. Pass through large rushy area to gate on R of this junction. **13** Here go on along small path just R of a faint track. When near next gate (and shed) bear over to it. **14** On in 2 fields by walls on your R. **15** At far corner of second field go through the L of 2 gates and across field to far corner. Here through 3 gates, R through farmyard and L along lane. Finally R at junction.

3A Alternative ascent making walk 1 km (¾ mi) shorter. Follow 1 6 then stay on valley-side path. **A** When this wide path stops keep on by main stream on your L. Cross smaller streams coming

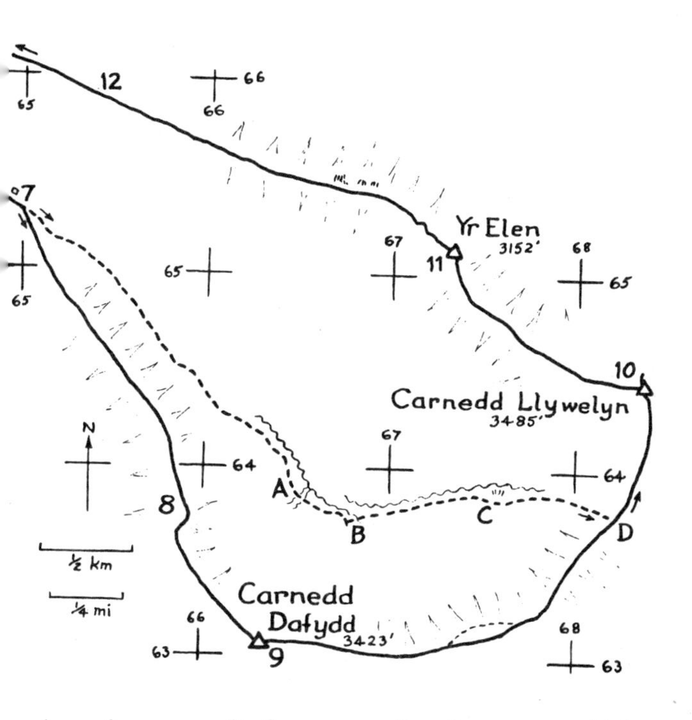

down from your R. Soon a small path appears which passes a large outcrop (6m high) and goes roughly E towards the col you are aiming for. (This col is grassy to its L and rocky to its R). **B** When path bears R and starts to approach a large marshy area turn L over stream up a pathless small grassy rise, on down a little and steeply up a boulder-strewn slope by a stream on your L. As gradient eases a small path appears, mostly about 5 m to R of stream. **C** Where outcrops are too close to the stream it is easier to bear a little away from the stream to where you are 10 m above it. (Almost no path now.) Go E to the col past aircraft wreckage. **D** Turn L along ridge to top of Carnedd Llywelyn. To return follow 10.

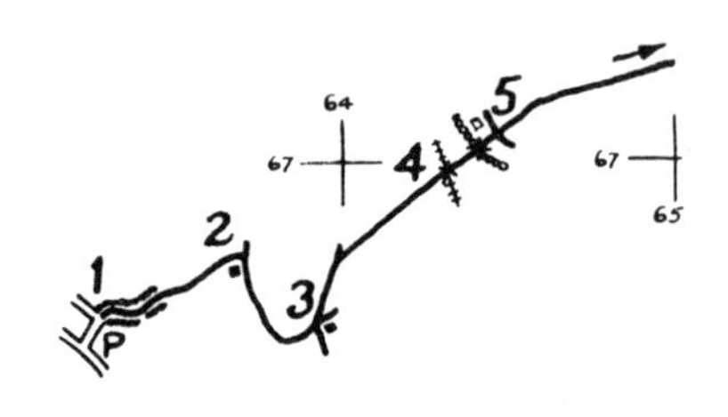

4 THE DROSGL RIDGE

(15.5 km, 9½ mi, 3200 ft) Map 115, S, CV

Summary. The gradients are quite gentle on this broad ridge which leads to the main Carneddau ridge. Fine views and the crags of Yr Elen are seen on the way along this ridge to Carnedd Llywelyn. After the first steep descent from Yr Elen the return is quite easy. Mist: the comments in walk 3 apply here.

Park in Gerlan as in walk 3.

1 Go to the top of Stryd Morgan and on up track between walls. After it bears R go L along grassy track (at first between walls) and on to gate just L of Cottage. **2** Turn R along track. It later swings L. **3** By a junction and building go one third L up a wide path for 200 m. Then fork R on path towards distant stile. Where path forks into 3 the L of these paths is perhaps best. **4** On over stile on fence (50 m R of crest of ridge) to stile in wall. **5** On up ridge (NE). Mostly no path, but easy.

6 At the spikey outcrops enjoy a short rocky ridge walk L (N) along them before going R (NE) up main ridge again towards distant tracks. **7** Here go on (E) up track nearest ridge crest, but leave it as it becomes level to bear L to the flat bouldery top of Drosgl. **8** Here go E/SE along the crest to Bera Bach, the next large rocky outcrop. **9** Here go on along nearly level section.

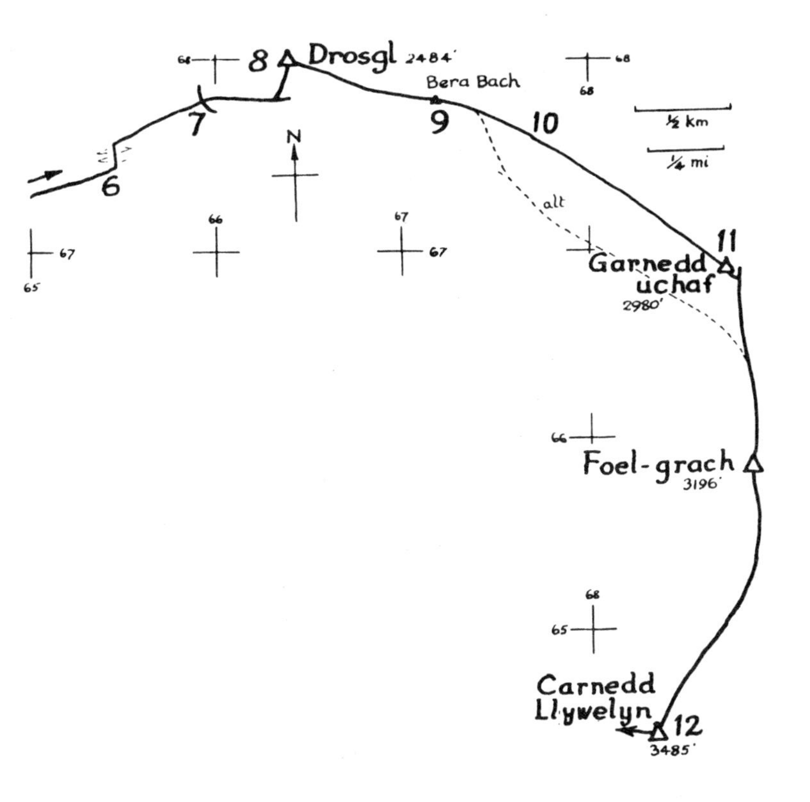

There is a path slightly R of ridge top. It will soon fade. (If you prefer a path one can be seen from Bera Bach. It goes along R side of ridge and is easily reached by a slight descent. It is marked by upright stones. It bypasses Garnedd uchaf). **10** On up ridge dodging boulder patches where you can until Garnedd uchaf is reached on the main ridge. **11** Here go on 50 m and turn R (S) along clear ridge path to Foel Grach and Carnedd Llywelyn. **12** Here turn R (W) to low jagged outcrops etc, as described in walk 3 from point 10 on.

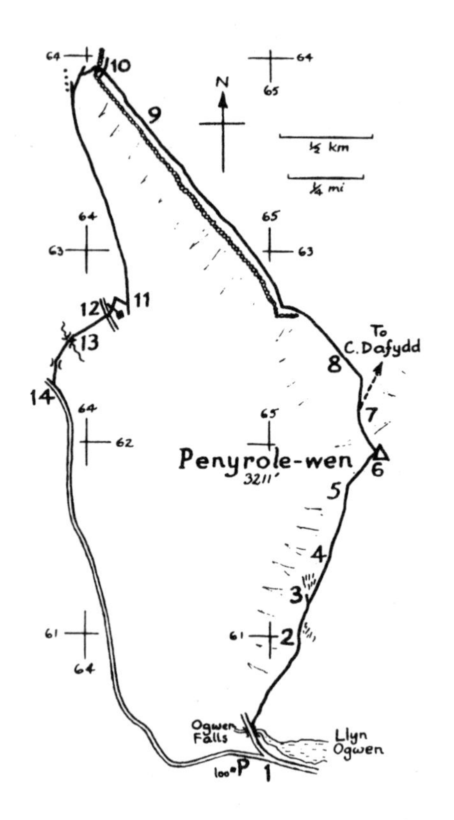

5 PENYROLE-WEN

(9 km, 5¾ mi, 2500 ft) Map 115, S

Summary. This direct route is very rough and steep in places with scrambles. (Average gradient 1 in 2!) But there are magnificent views to enjoy while resting. Carnedd Dafydd can be visited (adding an extra 2 km (1½ mi). The descent down the ridge is quite easy. After crossing the valley the walk ends with a gentle climb up a lane, still with fine mountain views. The Ogwen Falls seen are worth a closer visit by leaving the A5 by the bridge. Also the medieval packhorse bridge under this bridge, best seen from the E side. A dry route except that the flattish section of the

descent ridge can have slightly wet patches. If mist comes after reaching the top you should find the descent ridge using compass quite easily. Steep ground is not far to your L, and there is a wall to follow later on.
Car park (or layby) on the A5 near W end of Llyn Ogwen (649 604).

1 From car park go L along A5 towards Bethesda. Just after bridge go R though wall gap. At once go two thirds L along path to a good rock scramble. **2** When near the highest point that has been seen from the start, the path bears L to climb bare ground steeply, with scree at times, going just L of fine outcrops. **3** Soon after this a smaller outcrop of rather jagged rock is seen, with paths appearing to go L and R of them. Keep to the R (one or two cairns). (If you fork L you reach the base of these rocks where there is a tough enclosed scramble. Care is needed as hand and footholds are sparse.) **4** When the steep section is over keep on up the ridge. At outcrops path bears a bit to their R and then goes up through boulders. The path is vague here. Follow the cairns, mostly 10 m or so away from the steep ground on your L (N/NE). **5** At large cairn go on to summit. **6** From top go NW to col with steep ground on your R. **7** At col keep on N on almost level ground, thus leaving path half L. After 100 m bear half L (NW) down pathless slope towards a long ridge wooded at its far end. **8** Make for and follow wall along the ridge top when it is met. At the level section a path appears. **9** Descend to stile near gate. (Use the small path starting a few m R of wall.) **10** Over stile and half L (relative to direction stile points) down 100 m to a grassy wide path. Go L down it, soon joining the main path (marked by rushes and a line of stones on its far side). **11** Above farm in pines go sharp R down path to gate. There go L (with fence on your R) over drive to small gate. **12** Over road, through small gate and on to bridge. **13** Over bridge and half L by wall to outcrop. Here bear L over small bridge and on to road. **14** Go L up road.

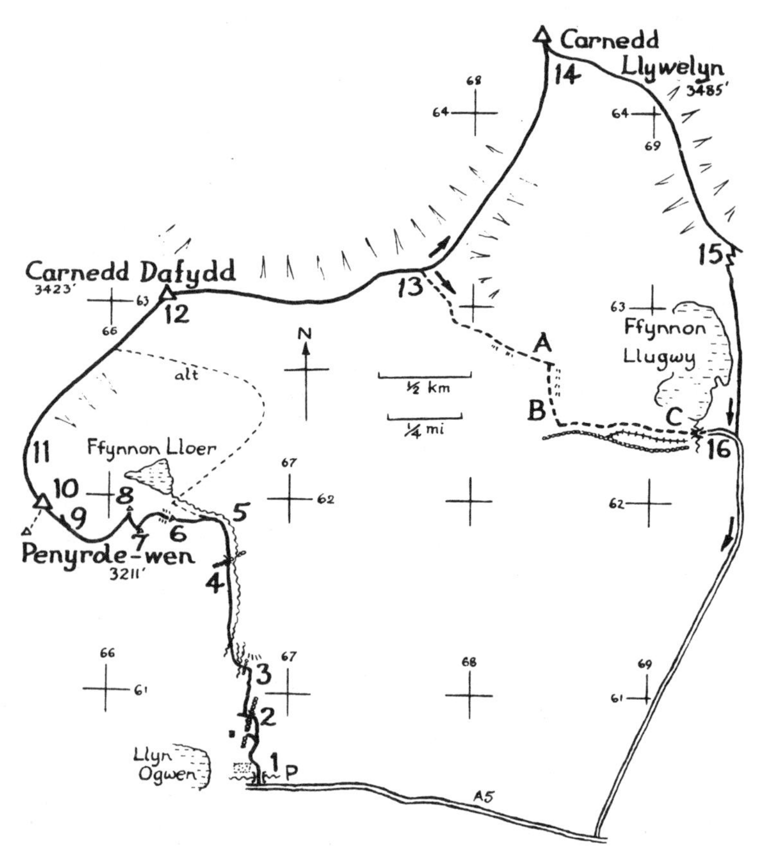

6 THE CARNEDDAU FROM THE A5

(14 km, 8¾ mi, 3100 ft) Map 115, S, CV

1 Go N over bridge along track past pines. 80 m before farmhouse turn R up path with wall on your L. **2** Over wall stile, on 15 m, and R up path. On up grass. Path at first vague and with wet patches. Aim for clear grass path in bracken seen ahead. **3** This path bears L as it nears an outcrop and soon goes through low wall gap to stream. Over stream and up near it, passing 15 m L of waterfall. Soon another stream is crossed and path becomes clearer. **4** Over stile and on near stream on your R. **5** 200 m after stile leave path and bear L up ridge unless you wish to avoid Penyrole-wen. (To avoid it keep on by stream until 50 m from lake. Then turn R up a small hummocky ridge. A small path may be met. Later bear L up grass to walk just above scree patches on the slopes above the lake. Turn R up ridge to summit and follow stages 12 and on.) **6** Scramble up a rocky gully with cairn below it and on along path. **7** At cairn follow path R thus getting back to crest of ridge. **8** At cairn (5 m before good view of lake) go sharp L with path. **9** Near top ignore path bearing R along the steep NE side of peak. Keep on to summit. **10** For views visit the cairn 200 m SW. From summit go NW to col with steep ground on your R. **11** At col go NNE along ridge passing L of 2 huge ancient cairns before reaching Carnedd Dafydd. **12** On E along ridge near steep ground on your L. **13** ● When Ffynnon Llugwy is seen to the E you can start the alternative descent (see below) or keep on along narrow ridge and up to Carnedd Llywelyn. **14** Here turn back but follow path that bears L (SE) down a new ridge. **15** At the col turn R down the steep path to pass L of Ffynnon Llugwy. (Or go on and scramble steeply up to Penyrhelgi-du. Go half R (S) down ridge, and follow point 10 of walk 7). **16** On down road and R along A5.

6A Alternative easier descent, making walk 1.5 km (1 mi) shorter. Follow walk 6 to point 13. There go R (SE) down a grassy side ridge. A path runs down the R edge of a boulder patch and can be seen further down the ridge, where it runs on grass just L of rocky crest of ridge. **A** After a nearly flat section you reach a line of scattered rocks on the R just before path starts to drop more steeply. Just before these rocks go R (S) down pathless grass. **B** Make for wall and follow it down (on your R). Soon a path runs about 20 m L of fence. It avoids most of the damp patches. **C** Cross a wide dry channel and bridge to road. Follow road down to A5 and R along it.

Summary. This is the best of all the walks on this range and can be made quite easy by the variations given. First you climb beside Afon Lloer with its many cascades. Then a fine ascent of Penyrole-wen is made with one short scramble and glimpses of

Ffynnon Lloer. There are glorious views towards Llyn Idwal all the way. Next follows a long delightful ridge passing over Carnedd Dafydd, then Carnedd Llywelyn, Then the ridge narrows and can soon be left by taking a path steeply down past Ffynnon Llugwy. (Or, with a little extra effort Penyrhelgi-du may be climbed.) The walk ends along a surfaced track and the A5, but the grand views are still to be seen. Routes are dry except near Afon Lloer, where there can be a few wet patches. Penyrole-wen can be avoided by going R of Ffynnon Lloer (wet patches near lake) and the alternative return replaces the very steep drop to the reservoir by a shorter and less steep (though tedious) descent down tussocky grass. To avoid most of the A5 go L along first drive met and R along track soon after bridge.
Park by the A5 near the small pine wood 200 m E of Llyn Ogwen. (668 605)

7 THE SOUTHERN CARNEDDAU

(12 km, 7½ mi, 2400 ft) Map 115, CV

Summary. To avoid some of the wet or vague paths in this area, a path by a leat is used to reach the S end of Llyn Cowlyd. Though artificial, this large lake is a beautiful sight from the top of Pen Llithrig-y-wrach, reached by a climb without paths in some sections. (The route is not too easy to follow, but there are no problems if you bear L to keep off the steep slope down to Llyn Cowlyd. There may be a few wet patches.) A fine ridge takes you to Penyrhelgi-du from which descent is very easy, with good views of the Glyderau all the way. If mist comes at or after reaching the first peak it is better to carry on NW to the clearly defined ridge unless you are sure you can retrace the more difficult route back S.
Park (without blocking the gate) at bottom of the reservoir road on the A5 (688 603) 2 km (1¼ mi) E of the E end of Llyn Ogwen.

1 Go up reservoir road. **2** Turn R along path with leat on your L. **3** After contouring round Cam-Tal-y-braich go L across bridge to stile in fence corner. On along slight path with fence on your L. **4**

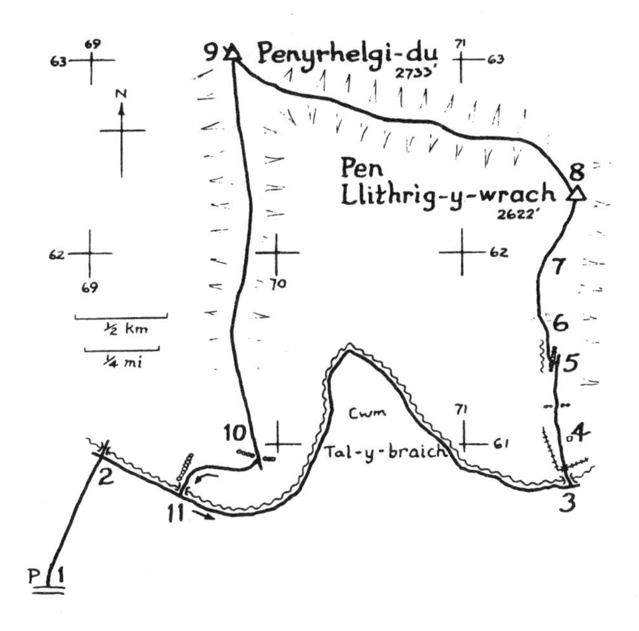

Close to a collapsed sheep fold on the R join a small path going N towards summit. It goes over low wall, up a short steep rise and over wettish patches. **5** Watch for a short length of fallen wall going up with a path beside it (on the R). Ignore this path and go L along another path which soon bears R and climbs beside stream on the L. **6** After a wet patch go NW up an obvious grass strip between rocks. Higher up, near some large rocks, it bears R (N) a little and the gradient eases. **7** When the rock-free grass/heather area is reached leave path and go up (NE) to the highest point. **8** Go N/NW down to the ridge and along path to Penyrhelgi-du. **9** Turn sharp L down ridge path. **10** Cross wall and follow path that bears R and runs parallel to A5 until 100 m from a wall. Then bear L down by a wall to bridge. **11** Cross bridge and go R along leat path.

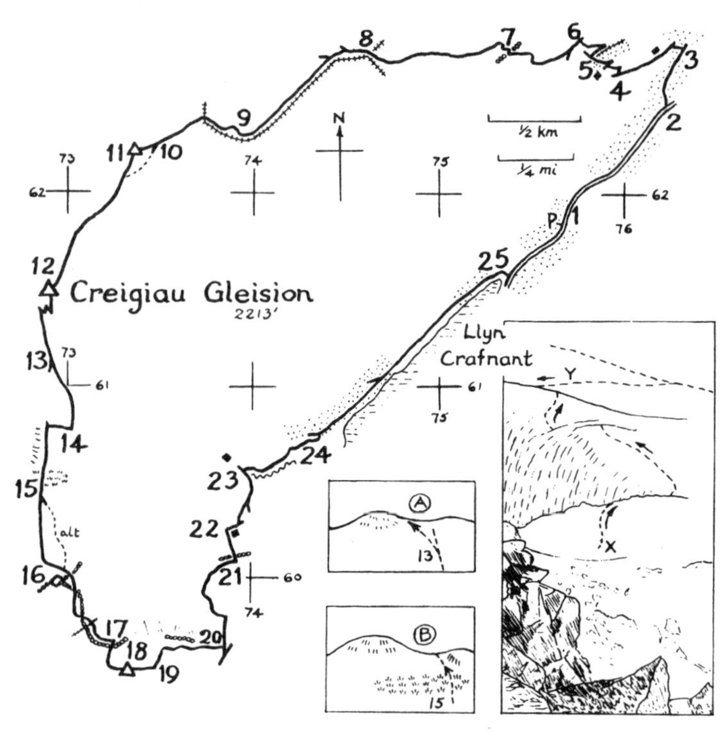

8 CREIGIAU GLEISION

(12.5 km, 7¾ mi, 2000 ft) Map 115, CV

1 Go back down road ¾ km (½ mi). **2** Fork L up lane. **3** After 300 m go L up clear path in wood to lane and L along it. Lane becomes a track after passing house. **4** Sharp R, sharp L with track. Again sharp R (50 m before gate) and sharp L. **5** Over gate and sharp R over grass with fence and wood on your R. (No path.) After 150 m go sharp L through bracken along the top edge of steepish slope. Soon you are by the R of a line of shrubs. Follow this line as it turns two thirds R just before you get near stream. **6** Turn L along clear track, soon taking a R fork up. **7** Through gate and up sunken path. **8** Through fence gap and on along path that bears L soon getting back beside fence. Ignore paths forking away from fence. Stay by fence. (Perhaps drier to L of fence.) **9** At steeper section clear path leaves fence for a while. Later path crosses fence where fence bends two thirds R. **10** At fork take path up to first summit. **11** Follow good path along ridge to summit. **12** On S along ridge path. Soon, at steep ground, it winds down on the R to flatter ground. Here turn L (S) along a clear path towards two hills. See small drawing A. **13** At fork near smaller hill fork L along path soon reaching the ridge of the rockier larger rise. **14** At steep drop path fades. Go 100 m to R and then L down small path towards marshy depression. Where it becomes vague keep on down to the marsh near small outcrops just to your R. See small drawing B. **15** Cross marsh on path which then rises gently passing 20 m to L of an outcrop on the smaller of 2 hills. The path soon runs clearly just below and R of outcrops on the rocky ridge. (Or climb up and carry on along a vague path on this ridge. The descent at the end is rough.) **16** The path bears L and goes down to wall and folds. Go through the wall, soon through wall again and along path by it until the path crosses back over wall again. On down to col. **17** Here go on along path that soon bears R to run beside wall (on your R). Follow wall (path fades soon) until it bears L and starts to descend at a col. Here go sharp R through low wall gap and take path curving L up to summit cairn. **18** Go on roughly E along path with steep ground not far to your L. **19** Soon there is steep ground ahead, with the view shown in the large drawing. Make for point X either directly or by first turning L down (towards lake) beside a tiny ridge for 50 m. Follow path down to Y with steep ground near your L. **20** At col go L along clear path. **21** Through gate in wall and over field to house. **22** Pass just L of house and turn R along track and soon L along path which soon joins track. **23** Turn R through gate (near house ahead). The path runs by stream and then through fields to stile. **24** Here go R along track. **25** Turn L down road.

Summary. On leaving the lane you start up a good scenic path to the ridge top. Then there is a level ½ mile which can be very wet, so the walk should be done in a dry season. At the lower summit fine views of Llyn Cowlyd and the mountains beyond it are first seen. The descent, which also may have some wet patches, carries on along the hummocky rocky ridge, part of which forms the background to so many pictures of Llyn Crafnant. From the col the Capel Curig — Crafnant path is used to reach the delightful return along the W side of the lake. Navigation

between points 13 and 20 could be difficult in mist, so it would be safer to turn back. Even in clear weather take care to follow the route described as paths are not too clear in some places.
Park in car park 400 m (¼ mi) before Llyn Crafnant is reached (754 618) (not free) or at N end of lake.

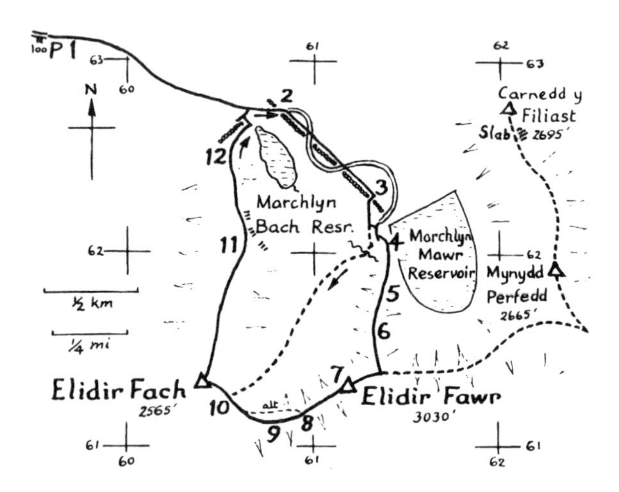

9 ELIDIR FAWR AND FACH

(7 km, 4¼ mi, 2000 ft) Map 115, S

Summary. An easy walk up to the now enlarged Marchlyn Mawr reservoir, followed by a choice of gentle or steep routes to Elidir Fawr. Either way the final summit is rough and bouldery, but this peak can be omitted if you wish. Elidir Fach is much smoother and the descent is easy with good views down to Marchlyn Bach reservoir and its crags. Being a short walk it can be linked with a visit to the N end of the Glyder range, adding 5 km (3 mi). The route is dry.

There is a fascinating geological exposure just S of Carnedd y Filiast, seen by going L just before the wall is met (622 626) after leaving this summit. It is a huge flat slab, tilted at a large angle, and showing a pattern of ripples dating back to the time when it once was a horizontal sandy sea shore.
Park at car park (595 631) at bottom of Marchlyn reservoir road 1.5 km (1 mi) E of Deiniolen.

1 Go up the road passing L of Marchlyn Bach reservoir. **2** Leave road and follow straight wall kept on your R. You cross the road twice. **3** At wall gap go half R through it and follow the dry channel. Cross it and climb up to road at any convenient place. **4** Near end of road go up the steep barren slope with steep ground and M Mawr reservoir on your L. **5** After a grassy stretch climb on up through boulders and up a small stony gully (with a flat tilted outcrop on its R). (This is rather near the edge. You may prefer to go up larger boulders on the R). **6** When the gradient eases go on (mainly over grass) to the cairn-like highest point in view. Here go 40 m to the path seen coming up. To visit Carnedd y Filiast go L along path to main ridge and sharp L along it. Otherwise go R along path to Elidir Fawr's summit. **7** On along the narrow bouldery ridge. **8** Soon after passing cairn on grassy strip going down to L you reach the next jumble of boulders. (If you wish to avoid these go half R along a small path going gently down and keeping a little below the boulders. It becomes vague at the crossing of a narrow strip of boulders, but it is easy to keep going on a short distance before bearing R down to the col. By using strips of grass you can avoid most the scree, and the slope is easy. At col follow 10.) Boulder lovers carry on along ridge. **9** When Llanberis and Llyn Padarn is seen go one third R away from ridge down a scree path (at first W) towards col. Use grassy strips to avoid most scree. **10** At col go on NW to Elidir Fach, then two thirds R (NNE) down broad ridge. **11** At clear path near top of crags bear L down it. Follow ridge down (N) to wall/fence. **12** R along by wall to road and back down it.

9A Easier ascent. Follow 1 to 3, but do not cross channel. Instead follow it to reach clear path down to stream and up valley to col. (Path fades on the way but walking is easy.) Here follow 10 to reach Elidir Fach or to climb Elidir Fawr first go L (SE) up easy but stony slopes. Use the curved grass strip to avoid most scree. When 50 m below crest bear L over easy scree below boulders, soon on small path taking you to the crest. (It avoids some, but not all of the boulders.) On to summit. Back the same way.

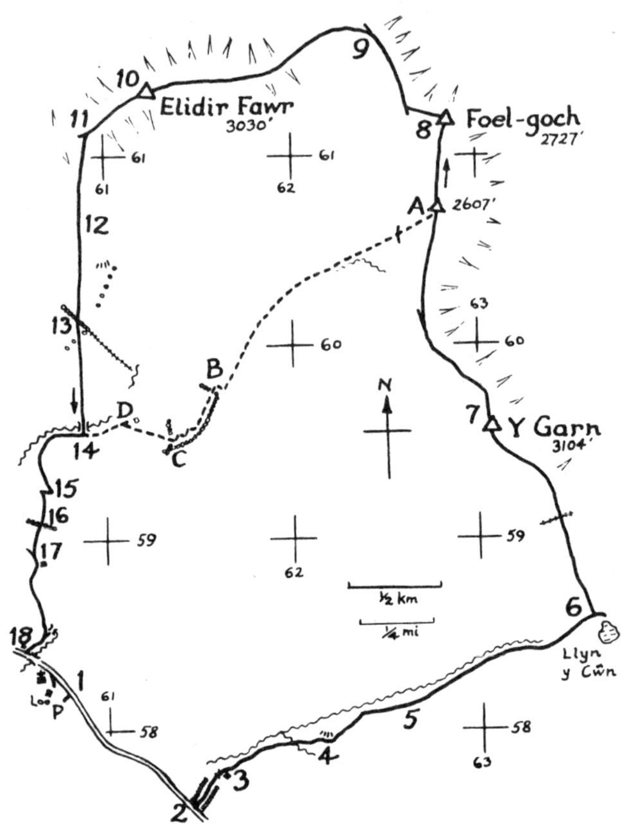

10 Y GARN TO ELIDIR FAWR FROM NANT PERIS

(12 km, 7½ mi, 3700 ft) Map 115, S

1 Turn R along road from car park. **2** Go L up track between walls. On up field. **3** Over stile. Up path by cottage. **4** After crossing stream scramble up rocks or bypass them to the R. **5** Follow path with fence and stream on your L. When path becomes vague and damp keep on E/NE. **6** At Llyn y Cwn turn L up path to Y Garn. ● **7** On along ridge to a nameless top (2607') and Foel-goch. **8** Here bear L, keeping steep ground by your R. Bear R along path to col. **9** Soon fork L along nearly level path which later climbs to Elidir Fawr. **10** Go on (SW) along bouldery ridge. **11** Watch for a grassy strip on L with a cairn at the top. Go L down grass and a small bare path. Carry on down roughly S towards green valley. You may find cairns and a faint path in places. **12** Look ahead where fence runs up from the stream (with remains of old wall beside it). Higher up it continues as a wall. Make for the stile in the wall near where fence ends. There are wet patches near stile most of which can be avoided. (If you veer too far left you should see a small outcrop and patch of boulders. There an old fallen wall leads you towards the stile.) **13** On over stile down path on a small ridge with stream on your R. **14** Over bridge and R down path. **15** Watch for sharp R turn. **16** Over stile and down to lane. **17** Follow lane L down to road. **18** Go L along road and half R along path just after church.

10A Alternative ascent omitting Y Garn (10 km, 6¼ mi, 3100 ft)
1 Take path on R of loo to road and L along it. **18** Turn R along lane by school. Keep on lane as it bears L just before a bridge. **17** Soon after cottage (Pant-y-fron) go half R up grass to stile. **16** On up path. **15** Follow path sharp R, sharp L. **D** 200 m past bridge leave path near old fold and go half R up to wall gap and on to join path up ridge by wall. **B** Over stile at wall end and up ridge. When all rocks have been passed go along faint path at first beside ditch. Then on to highest point. **A** L along ridge to Foel-goch. Here follow stage 8 etc.

10 B Alternative descent omitting Elidir Fawr (10 km, 6¼ mi, 2800 ft)
Follow 1 to 6 to reach Y Garn. **7** On along ridge to next summit (2607 ft). **A** Here go L down small ridge (just L of Llyn Peris). **B** Over stile and on with wall on your L. **C** After short steep descent cross remains of wall and go half R to wall gap. On to join good path near fold. **D** Along path past bridge. Now follow main walk 15 — 18.

Summary. An attractive but steep ascent reaches Llyn y Cwn near a col. In the final stages the path can be rather wet. You then start a splendid long ridge walk which bears left across a superb narrow col (with views of the reservoir) to Elidir Fawr. It goes on, very rough and bouldery, for a short distance before a fairly easy, though often pathless, descent. One wettish section may be

met. Fortunately the slate quarries on your R do not dominate the view, and instead the Snowdon range can be enjoyed. The alternative route along an attractive and little known ridge is useful for shorter walks. In mist there are no serious hazards if the Elidir Fawr ridge is left at the right place. If in doubt retreat to the alternative descent.
Park in Nant Peris car park (607 582) on the A4086.

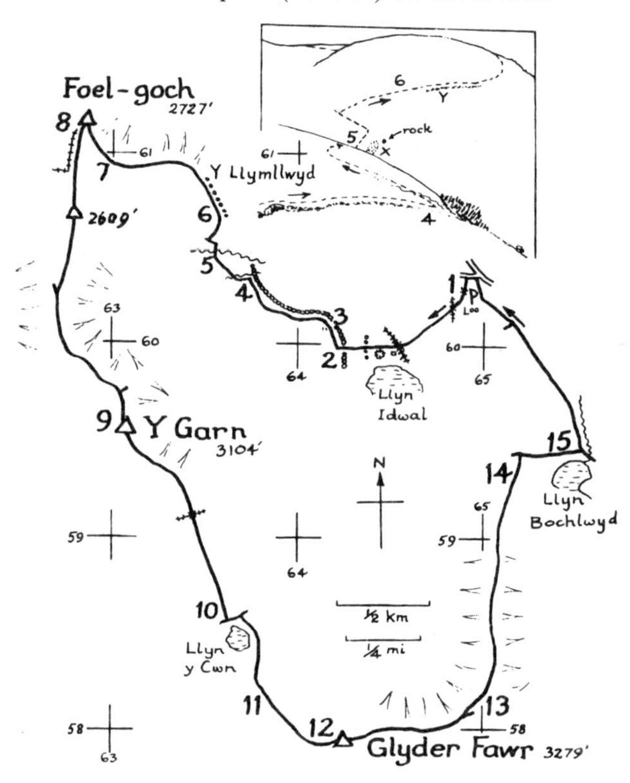

11 FOEL-GOCH TO GLYDER FAWR

(11 km, 6¾ mi, 3400 ft) Map 115, S

Summary. A little known route takes you near the impressive crags of Y Llymllwyd before reaching Foel-goch. Then follows a fine ridge walk with some ups and downs ending in a steep rough climb to Glyder Fawr. After the first steep section, descent to Llyn Bochlwyd is easy. Beyond this is another short rough steep descent. Varied and splendid views all the way. The walk can be shortened by leaving the ridge at 10 (see walk 13) or even (rather tediously) down the side ridge path 200 m N of Y Garn. Stages 4 to 6 are vague, and there can be wet patches near 1, 4 and 15. **Park** near the W end of Llyn Ogwen (649 603)

1 Go straight up path starting at R end of back of car park. After short steep rise go half L to stile and along path 100 m to next stile. Over this and half L again along vague path W/SW to cross small stile by large boulder. Go one third R on faint path passing just R of fenced enclosure. Soon through fallen wall and on to wall gap. **2** Through wall gap and R along by wall (on your R). **3** After a scramble (easily avoided to the L) wall bears L then R. At a slight descent a path bearing temporarily away from wall can be used. **4** At a stream 50 m before ravine seen ahead, go L up by stream (on your R) for 50 m. See drawing. Then bear R over slightly wet grass to reach stream and cross it about 30 m L of a bare reddish patch X. **5** Here go up grass and bear L keeping just below scree until a path is found slanting up R. It starts where the grass on your L changes to scree. This avoids most of the scree. (If you miss the path you can go up the easy slope anywhere.) **6** Carry on up the broad grassy ridge. There is a slight path beside an old wall Y. Make for R edge of ridge with crags below. A good path winds up here. **7** Cross bare patch at col then bear R up grass to Foel-goch. **8** Turn sharp L along main ridge with fence on your R. Go over summit 2609 ft and on to Y Garn. **9** On down, at first with steep ground just L, and then down path to Llyn y Cwn. **10** Turn L to pass just L of the lake. Just after passing turn R along path soon up rough steep scree path. **11** When gradient eases follow cairned path (with a final easy scramble) to Glyder Fawr. **12** Go E/NE towards outcrop 70 m away and follow cairned path. It soon bears R to avoid another outcrop. On (E) towards Glyder Fach. (Vague path.) Make for line of cairns for easier crossing of flat bouldery area. At grass bear L keeping steep ground near your L. **13** At a side ridge here descend steep rocky ground (path at times) to an easy clear path down ridge. **14** Near bottom of ridge go R to stream at L end of Llyn Bochlwyd. **15** Here L down clear rough path at first by stream. Later it is less clear and can be a bit wet. Aim for the L end of Llyn Ogwen to join a good path back.

12 Y GARN TO GLYDER FACH

(11 km, 6¾ mi, 3200 ft) Map 115, S

Summary. A rough path takes you up an enjoyable side ridge. This reaches the main ridge not far from the top of Y Garn. The first Glyder is reached after a steep rough climb starting near a small lake. After a grassy section comes a remarkable area of outcrops and boulders. The summit is a heap of huge boulders on a large flat area. Nearby is the Cantilever. Soon you pass the top of Bristly ridge and descend gently (still with patches of boulders) to a grassy area. Here the Miners' Track takes you back past Llyn Bochlwyd. It is rough in places but not steep, except for one short section. This splendid walk includes all the outstanding features of the ridge. It is rough and steep in parts, with one or two easy scrambles, and plenty of clambering over boulders. The grass can be rather wet in stages 1 and 15. The walk can be shortened by going down E/NE at 6 (see walk 13, stage 20) or 8 (walk 11 stage 12). Glyder Fach should be avoided if in mist.

Park near the W end of Llyn Ogwen (649 603).

1 Go straight up path starting at R end of back of car park. After short steep rise go half L to stile and along path 100 m to next stile. Over this and half L along vague path W/SW to cross small stile by large boulder. Go one third R on faint path passing just R of fenced enclosure. Soon through fallen wall and on to wall gap. **2** Here go one third R (NW) 100 m to solitary iron post, at which a rough path starts. It bears R to a clear path. **3** Near Llyn Clyd it bears R. **4** At main ridge go L to Y Garn. **5** On down, at first with steep ground just L, and then down path to Llyn y Cwn. **6** Turn left to pass just L of the lake. Just after passing it turn R along path soon up a rough steep scree path. **7** When gradient eases follow cairned path (with final easy scramble) to Glyder Fawr. **8** Go E/NE towards outcrop 70 m away and follow cairned path. It soon bears R to avoid another outcrop. On (E) towards Glyder Fach. (Vague path.) Make for line of cairns for an easier crossing

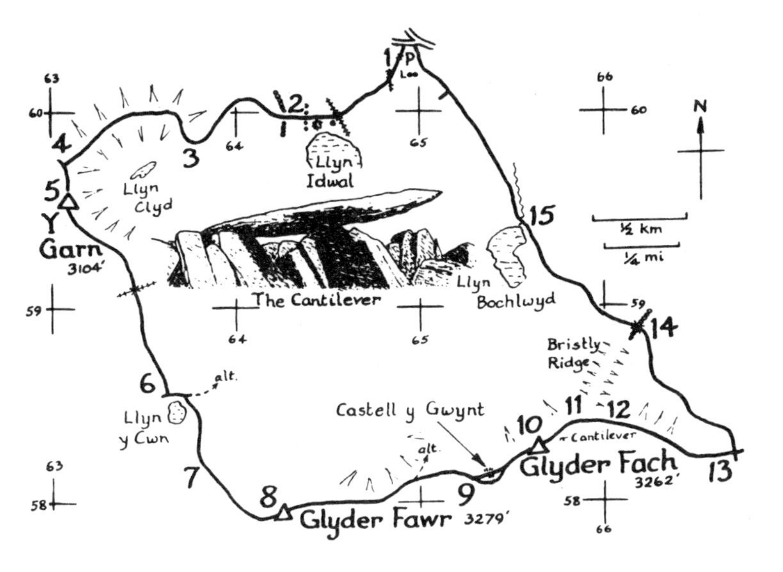

of flat bouldery area. On over grass, a cairned rocky section and a level path over grass slope to boulders. **9** Here you can either go straight through the jagged outcrop Castell y Gwynt or try to follow the path R of it. Both routes meet plenty of boulders before the summit of Glyder Fach, itself a pile of huge boulders, is reached. (It rests on a large flat area and can be bypassed.) **10** Go on (NE) over the flat area, soon reaching Bristly Ridge, a rocky ridge leaving L of the main ridge. **11** Ignore this and go roughly E down a bouldery area. It has cairns, but there is hardly any path. **12** Carry on down path at an easier gradient, with steep ground not far to the L. **13** 200 m before a lake, the Miners' Track crosses your path. Go L down this. It bears L and reaches the col just below Bristly Ridge after bearing R to dodge most of a patch of boulders. **14** Here go over stile and down to Llyn Bochlwyd. **15** On down by stream (on your R) at first. Path becomes less clear and can be a bit wet. Aim for the L end of Llyn Ogwen to join a good path back.

13 TRYFAN AND GLYDER FACH AND FAWR

(9.5 km, 6 mi, 3100 ft) Map 115, S

Summary. This is the toughest walk in the book — steep, rough and with plenty of scrambles. So don't try it until you know you enjoy this kind of walking. It starts up the dreaded N ridge of Tryfan. However, if the route is carefully followed, all the scrambles are reassuringly enclosed. (If you miss your way you should still reach the cairn described in stage 8, where the ridge crest is left for an easier route on the side.) After an easier but bouldery descent Bristly Ridge is another rocky and scrambly section. When Glyder Fach and Fawr are reached the ground is flatter but still bouldery in places. Then follows a steep rough descent passing below the Devil's Kitchen, a remarkable gully, before the attractive return past Llyn Idwal. A spectacular and unforgettable route. By omitting Glyder Fawr an easier descent, can be made. The wide Glyderau ridge could be confusing in mist. If caught by mist on Bristly Ridge it would be best to reach its top and turn L down to the Miners' track as in walk 12 stage 11. To return from the bottom of this ridge use walk 12 from stage 14.

Park in the first layby on L (664 603) after reaching Llyn Ogwen from Capel Curig.

1 Over stile and half R up path, soon by wall. **2** Path turns half L 50 m before wall ends at crag. It soon reaches crag base. Follow paths keeping within 10 m from crag base (on your R). When a rock outcrop sticks out in your way scramble over it (or detour round it). You will probably find the other scrambles you meet are no harder than this one. Soon scramble up a second outcrop that sticks out. See drawing A. Then on again within 10 m of smaller crag bases. **3** Take nearly level path in heather (E/NE) at first aiming just right of perched boulder. (Drawing B). 50 m past the corner shown you reach boulders. Use path in heather on their R to avoid them. Soon on again within 10 m of crag bases. **4** After big boulder on your L watch for bigger one with tree to its R. (Drawing C.) Pass 10 m to L of bigger boulder and bear R (S/SW)

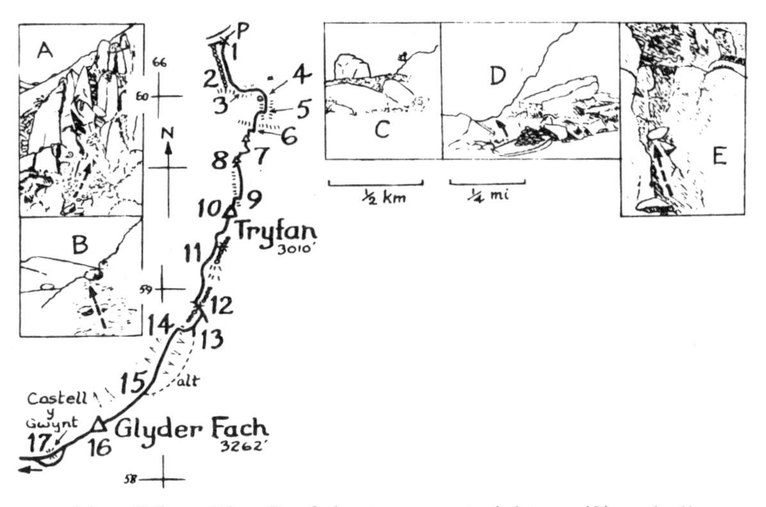

up ridge. When 15 m L of the tree go straight up (S) a shallow bouldery gully between rocks. **5** After 10 m it steepens, so go R on path which bears L to go up just R of gully. Keep on as straight up as the terrain allows. (Vague paths.) Make for the R end of a wide spread of outcrops ahead. Then make for the slight dip between these and some more outcrops to the right which come into view. **6** When the scramble becomes more like a rock climb scramble R to the skyline and L to large cairn on an area of flat ground. On S/SE up cairned route near ridge crest. **7** When you reach large outcrops take cairned path L soon bearing R to get above them. On again near crest. **8** Watch for cairn on 3 m long flat boulder. (Drawing D.) Here go on (S) between rocks and down 15 m to join clear cairned path up side of ridge. Later it is level along crag base, then up steeply (scramble), down, level again along crag base. **9** 10 m before a 2½ m rock blocks path go R up gully and under a rock 'bridge'. Then scramble L out of gully and up boulders 100 m to summit. **10** Go on down bouldery ridge. Avoid steep section near stiles on a col by a detour R. **11** At col a path goes down keeping R of the rocky crest. **12** At next col cross wall by stile and go up path in scree not far from wall. **13** After 100 m you could fork L steeply up scree L of ridge or better fork R along path towards ridge which is reached by going up

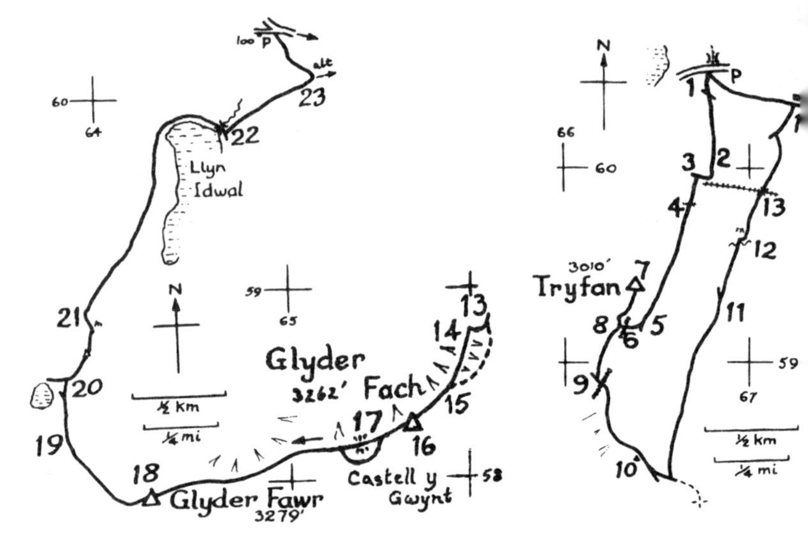

gully when path ends. 5 m before boulders bar the route scramble R to crest. **14** Up ridge passing just R of the first vertical rockface. The path starts to descend, but leave it and keep just R of crest past the next obstacle. You should reach a large sloping slab with quartz patches. Here take a level course past rocks on your L to reach gully. (See drawing E.) Go half L up it and R up boot-worn rocks to crest. At next very steep rocks go round their base to the R. Over boulders and slightly down to an easy path that takes you up to crest for a final easy section. **15** On (SW) to summit. **16** On (SW) over flattish area to the spiky outcrop (Castell y Gwynt). **17** Pass just L or through it and down to clear path. On up to Glyder Fawr.

18 On down cairned path that bears R (NW). **19** Half R down steep rough path that reaches flat ground just R of Llyn y Cŵn. **20** Here take path half R (E/NE) to a large cairn. There down beside scree, and later down grass until a crag forces you to the L. **21** Here pick your way down a bouldery slope. Watch for the start of the steps. (They end at one point but start again a little lower down.) **22** Round lake past bridge and L along stony path. **23** Where it turns L you can make a pathless short cut E/NE to road. It can be wet in places. Otherwise return along road.

14 TRYFAN THE EASY WAY

(6 km, 3¾ mi, 2000 fti) Map 115, S

Summary. Heather Terrace is a rough but not steep route on the E side of Tryfan. After this a clamber up boulders brings you to the summit. When clear of the boulders all that is left is an easy valley descent which is mainly dry and passes through masses of heather. (Braich y Ddeugwm makes a good ridge descent but involves crossing a marshy area near Llyn y Caseg-fraith.)

Park near bridge (668 605) 250 m E of the E end of Llyn Ogwen.

1 Over the stile almost opposite bridge. Ignore the track and at once take the path going up half R from it. Soon on over a crossing path. **2** When the route starts to get vague with several choices, keep on with tilted outcrops just to your L, towards fence. Soon go R on clear path which leads to an easy scramble up between rocks. **3** After this at once turn L along a small path which crosses a stream after 20 m. Keep on with steep ground on your L. **4** At a scree shoot a firm path goes up diagonally across it. Later the path runs up an obvious wide shelf on the side of Tryfan. **5** When a new view is seen ahead (Bristly Ridge) the path starts to go down. 30 m after start of drop, fork R up a grassy strip to a wall. **6** Here go over stile and R up boulders to top. Use cairned 'paths' if you like, though these are hardly better than choosing your own route. **7** Return the same way to 6. **8** Here take path that keeps R of the rocky ridge and goes down to col. **9** Here turn L on path (Miners' Track) which soon goes just L of most of the boulders of a bouldery area. **10** After slight rise to cairn on boulder note fork 150 m ahead. Take the L fork for 70 m until just past a long narrow scree strip. Then sharp L down grass path between scree and stream. Make for the clear path going N/NE on flattish ground near the steep side of Tryfan. **11** At fork take R fork down. Soon a grassy wettish patch is met for 50 m before path becomes bare again. **12** Near a rocky rise, path crosses stream and goes quite steeply down thus passing to R of this rise. **13** Over fence stile and on down path. Later a larger path on flat low outcrop is joined. **14** Just before buildings turn L along track.

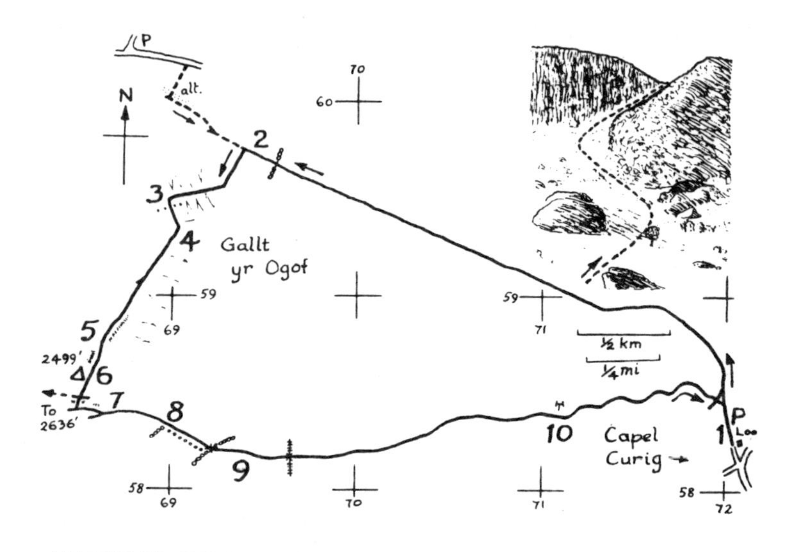

15 THE SOUTH EAST GLYDERAU

(9.5 km, 6 mi, 1900 ft) Map 115 CV, (S)

Summary. This end of the range is gentler country making walking easy. There is a stiff climb, though, up the impressive Gallt yr Ogof. Then follows an attractive ridge which joins the main wider ridge, down which you return to Capel Curig. The flat parts have wet section in some seasons. Stage 10 has vague paths, but any route E that dodges outcrops is unlikely to cause difficulties. If you wish to get climbing sooner, park at the reservoir road end (688 603). Then go 300 m towards Capel Curig and turn R along footpath then L along track. 200 m before stile and gate follow 2.

Park at Capel Curig car park off minor turning past loos (721 581).

1 Continue N along this turning. Keep on for over 3 km (2 mi). **2** 200 m after stile and gate in wall, turn L (SW) up dry grass when 300 m before a group of pines. Make for the bottom of the large gully that slopes up from L to R. See drawing. At gully follow faint path just L of stream. Bear L at top of scree patch along the edge of heather until 10 m before rock. Then go R up path in heather. Where path reaches a rocky section keep near stream after going up a rock step. At the top of easily avoided scree a path in heather about 10 m R of gully outcrop gets you to an easier gradient. Here on up without path. **3** When line of posts is seen leading back along top of gully turn L (S/SE) past them up grass with scattered small outcrops. Steep ground is not far from your L. **4** At crest, bear R up ridge. Soon a path appears. Where path sneaks round on R of highest part of ridge, take the L fork that keeps nearest to the top, but just avoids the boulders. **5** Soon path bears L across a grassy section of the ridge so the next boulders are kept just R of path. (One short patch of boulders has to be crossed.) **6** Just before path descends visit large summit cairn 15 m to R of path. On down path (SW, towards Y Lliwedd) for 100 m to a crossing path. (At this point the walk can be extended by going roughly SW to the nameless peak 2636 ft and back.) Go down grass more steeply (no path) between 2 small outcrops, then L along a fairly level path. Keep on if it becomes vague and you will soon see it again along base of a large flat tilted rock slab. **7** Here make for clear path 20 m ahead and go half L along it. **8** Down just L of broken wall and over stile. **9** Carry on along ridge. Path forks at 2 places. Try the L forks, but avoid any paths that seem to be leaving the ridge. **10** Near a TV aerial old red spots mark the route. Go on (E) and join a path that seems to be bearing L off ridge. It soon turns back again. Hunt spots down to reach the track you came along just L of farm.

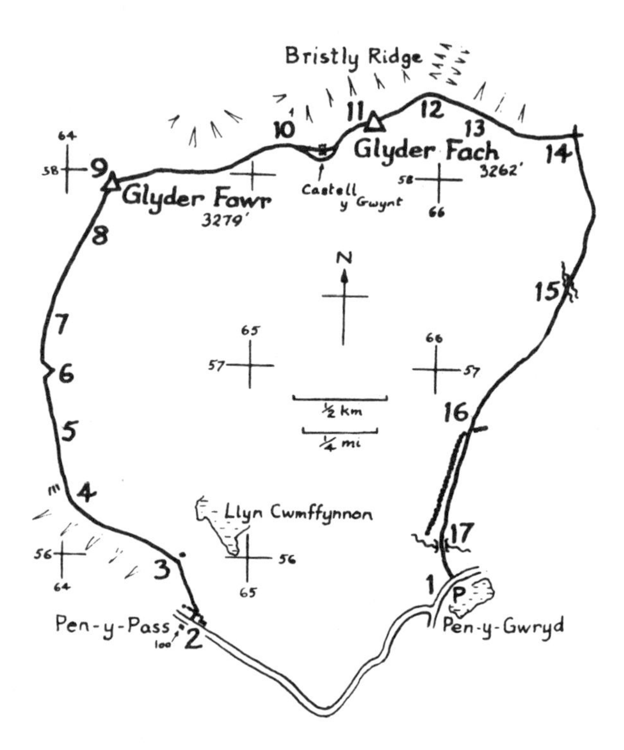

16 THE GLYDERAU FROM PEN-Y-GWRYD

(10 km, 6½ mi, 2600 ft) Map 115, S

Summary. After a road walk to the pass the ascent is quite easy and marked by red spots. The attractive Llyn Cwmffynnon is seen early on. Looking back there are fine views of the Snowdon range. Then follows the remarkable ridge with its impressive rocks and patches of unavoidable boulders. Descent by the Miners' Track is at a gentle gradient but it is very rough in places. Usually dry though sometimes wettish after point 3. Don't go on if the ridge is in mist as it can be confusing.

Park in layby near Pen-y-Gwryd (661 559)

1 Walk to the road junction and up the A4086 to top of pass (Pen-y-Pass). **2** Just past hostel (on R) turn R though gate and on to stile. Go half L up path marked by red spots. **3** By large (4 m) boulder at top of rise bear L to contour round tiny hillock on your L and pick up path down to small pool. (Not to Llyn Cwmffynnon.) On over a small marshy area to more spots and clear path. **4** Path steepens as it bears R to avoid large outcrop ahead. **5** When gradient eases keep on (N) up wide ridge. **6** At steeper section zig-zag round scree. **7** On N/NE when ridge comes into view and gradient eases. (Path makes for Glyder Fawr, the second peak from the L.) **8** Final easy climb up path in boulders to summit. **9** Go E/NE towards outcrop 70m away and take cairned path which soon curves R to avoid another outcrop. On (E) towards the next Glyder. (Path vague.) Make for a line of cairns marking slightly easier crossing of flat area of small boulders. On over grass, a cairned rocky section and a level path across a grass slope. **10** Here go straight through the jagged outcrop Castell y Gwynt or try to follow path R of it. Both routes meet many boulders before reaching Glyder Fach, itself a pile of huge boulders. (They are on large flat area and can be bypassed.) **11** Go on (NE) over flat area, soon reaching Bristly Ridge, a rocky ridge leaving L of the main ridge. **12** Ignore this and go roughly E down bouldery area. It has cairns but hardly any path. **13** On down path at easier gradient with steep ground not far to the L. **14** 200 m before lake turn R along path (Miners' Track). **15** Cross 2 streams near waterfall. On towards lake near road junction. **16** Through wall gap and on with wall on your R. **17** Over stile and bridge. Half L to road.

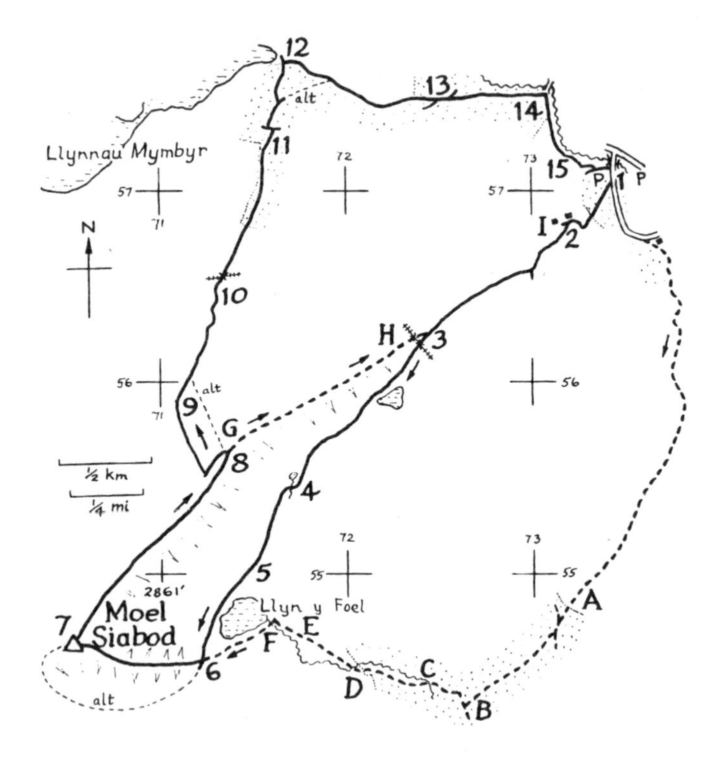

17 MOEL SIABOD

(10.5 km, 6½ mi, 2500 ft) Map 115, CV

Summary. After a gentle start up to the beautiful Llyn y Foel a delightful steep rocky ridge with easy scrambles takes you right to the top. Then there is a fine rocky ridge to enjoy before the easy grassy descent towards Llynnau Mymbyr. After the pine wood there is a pleasant return first along the edge of natural woodland and then beside a lovely river. The alternative ascent starts in woodland, crosses moorland to a plantation and makes a good rocky ascent beside an attractive mountain stream. In mist the main descent should not cause problems using a compass. Ground can be rather wet in places between 3 and 6.

Park just up minor road (734 571) leaving A5 just over 1.5 km (1 mi) from Capel Curig road junction, or in layby on A5.

1 Go on along minor road a few m, and turn half R up surfaced drive. **2** At buildings, go half L up rough track. After 300 m ignore turning L to nearby gate. **3** On over the L of 2 stiles (50 m apart) in fence. (Soon a small wet patch just before a pool can be avoided by a short detour R.) **4** Pass just L of huge water filled hole at mine. Bear R round hole on small path over small stream. Path soon bears L (SW) gently climbing. It soon runs just below heather on its R. **5** Near Llyn y Foel go on over wettish ground to cairn at start of ridge. **6** Go W up cairned path on ridge. Finally up boulders to top. (To avoid this ridge keep on at 6 until you can go up easier grassy slope on the R). **7** Go R (NE) down grass to what seems a second top, and on down rocky ridge. Detour L to get round a small drop in the ridge. **8** At the end of outcrops and boulders, either go down pathless grass towards Llynnau Mymbyr or go back on grass beside ridge 150 m and R down path. **9** Later aim towards R end of the 2 lakes to reach a tiny ridge where a clear path winds down. **10** Over stile and on. **11** At forest road go L 20 m then R. Turn L after 100m. **12** Go R along track. **13** Ignore track forking L. **14** Don't cross bridge. Turn R along riverside. **15** Through fence gap and L along track.

17A Alternative ascent and descent (10 km, 6¼ mi, 2500 ft)
1 Go on along minor road 400m, then half R up stony track between house and fence. **A** Into wood, soon ignoring a sharp R turn off. Take R turn soon after this. **B** Turn R at junction. **C** When track ends go L across stream and up path in trees, with stream not far R. (Waterfall soon.) **D** Over stile out of wood along path 50m to stream. Cross stream and follow path on R of stream. Leave stream as it bears L to a gorge. On up path. **E** Stream gets back to path, which becomes bouldery and has an easy scramble. (Avoid final wettish patch by detour R.) **F** At lake go L over dam and along path to cairn at start of final ridge. Follow 6 and 7. **G** 50 m past end of boulders a cairned path goes down NE, then bearing slightly R. On down with steep ground near your R. **H** Over stile and down track. **I** R down drive.

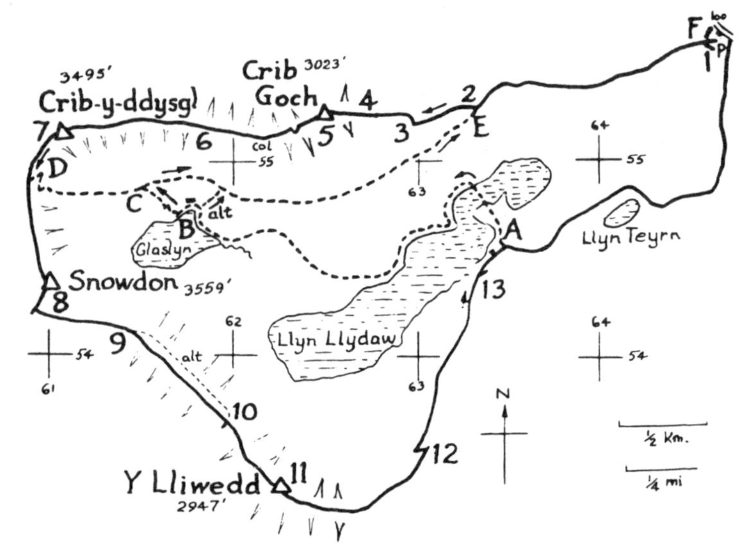

18 THE SNOWDON HORSESHOE

(11.5 km, 7¼ mi, 3,300 ft) Map 115, S

Summary. An exceptionally fine ridge walk with some scrambles on the narrow rocky ridge around Crib Goch. Only the descent from the summit is rather tedious, being steep and rough, but the spendid views compensate for this. Then follows the enjoyable rough traverse of Y Lliwedd before the final return. Avoid this walk in strong winds or if not an experienced scrambler. The alternative routes up the Miners' and down the Pig Track are also very good. They go along the side of the ridge and are free of scrambles and other difficulties, though there is one short rough steep ascent. This steep ascent can be avoided by going NE up grass at Glaslyn to reach the Pig Track.

Park (only free out of season) at Pen-y-Pass (648 556)

1 Take path at R end of rear of car park (as seen from road). Soon through wall gap. **2** At col where Llyn Llydaw is first seen fork R up path, at first by fence. **3** After path climbs side of hill, take the obvious R turn steeply up scree, then rocks. Soon path levels.

Keep on by cairns, soon bearing L. **4** Go straight up steepening ground keeping near cairns. (Several scrambly routes possible.) Keep on the final narrow rocky crest up to top. **5** On along crest. When it rises to a pinnacle go along the L base of it to a small dip. Here scramble steeply up rock and on along ridge. **6** After col more scrambling. **7** Bear L to summit. **8** On down path to grassy, less steep area where stone marks Watkin path. Go L down steep rough path. **9** When level it goes on below ridge crest. (Move on to crest for better views.) **10** Climb Y Lliwedd, keeping fairly near L for views. Some scrambling. **11** Follow path down. **12** Descend rough path towards Llyn Llydaw. Use zig-zag L to an outcrop, then sharp R. **13** 100 m before hut fork L to pass just R of hut. Soon R along track.

18A Alternative easier walk (12 km, 7½ mi, 2500 ft)
1 From car park go along nearly level track S. **A** Near second lake fork R, soon crossing its causeway. **B** Just after ruin by third lake go one third R at large cairn up easy scree to rough path bearing R. Soon cross to a parallel cairned path 20 m to L. It bears L to go through gap in the line of outcrops on the L. **C** On when upper path is reached. **D** At top of zig-zags bear L to summit. Turn back to point C then stay on upper nearly level path. **E** At col go on down clear path. **F** Through wall gap to car park.

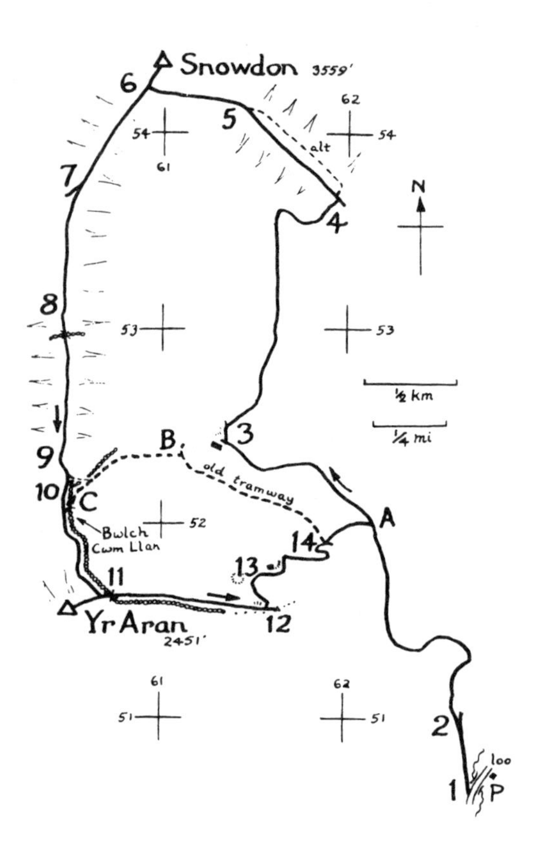

19. SNOWDON AND YR ARAN

(13.5 km, 8½ mi, 4300 ft) Map 115, S

Summary. The ascent uses the Watkin Path with many lovely waterfalls in the early stages. It is quite easy until the final steep rough section. Then follows a fine gently descending ridge with a short rough steeper ending at Bwlch Cwm Llan. The rise to the craggy Yr Aran and its E ridge is well worth the effort, but can be omitted.

Park at Pont Bethania (628 507) on A498 km (3 mi) NE of Beddgelert.

1 Cross bridge and turn sharp R (N) along drive, at first near river. **2** Fork half L up stony track. ● **3** At mine building track bears R to pass just R of mine tip. Soon R along main path where smaller path goes straight on. **4** Turn L at T-junction. (Or go on up to crest of ridge and L for better views.) **5** On (W/NW) up steep bare path that aims L of summit. **6** R up to summit and back. Then on down ridge. **7** Take L fork gently up. **8** 100 m before wall the scree can mostly be avoided either on grass R or rock L. **9** Follow cairn to R for final descent to col. (Here Yr Aran can be omitted by going down to the old tramway. Paths vague and can be wet. Perhaps it is best to bear L just before col down rough scree path through wall gap. Keep by wall for 100 m or so, then go E down grass to upright slates where tramway is joined.) **10** At col keep on along path near wall (on your L). **11** On reaching ridge go sharp R to top and back. Then over stile and down ridge by wall on your R. **12** After final old fence post in view, go on 50 m to cairn for view. (Here more posts are seen going steeply down.) Turn back to that post and go R (N/NE) down grass passing just R of nearest outcrop. Soon bear L (N/NW) down grass to waste tip beside large quarry hole. **13** Here bear R to ruin and second rust-coloured tip. Pass just R of tip and bear L on faint path round tip. 80 m below tip a 5 m length of wall marks the start of a track. Go R (E/NE) down it. **14** After sharp turns L then R, go half L down path to rejoin Watkin Path.

19A Yr Aran alone (9 km, 5½ mi, 2300 ft)

Follow walk 19 stages 1 and 2. **A** When track stops rising go half L up clear path. Turn R along level track (old tramway). **B** As it bends R near old mine, go L up grass to join path by wall. **C** At col keep L of walls until stile is reached. Then cross wall and follow walk 19 stage 10.

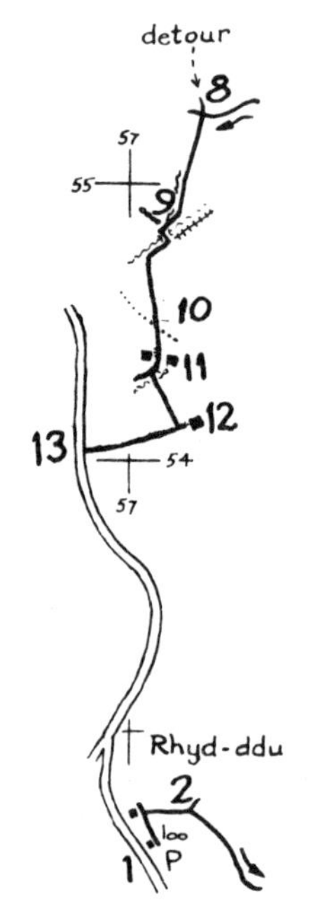

20 SNOWDON FROM RHYD-DDU

(14 km, 8¾ mi, 3000 ft) Map 115, S

Summary. After a gentle start fine views are seen from a side ridge (Llechog) before the excellent main ridge takes you to the summit. The Ranger path takes you down another good side ridge. The best return would use the old railway track, but at the moment it is not a right of way, so a road walk is necessary. Llyn Cwellyn and many other smaller lakes enhance the views of this walk. There may be a wettish patch on the lower section of the Ranger path.

Park just S of Rhyd-ddu (571 526)

1 Take track past loo for 100 m to house, then turn R. **2** After 200 m fork R. **3** After going through several walls, turn L through

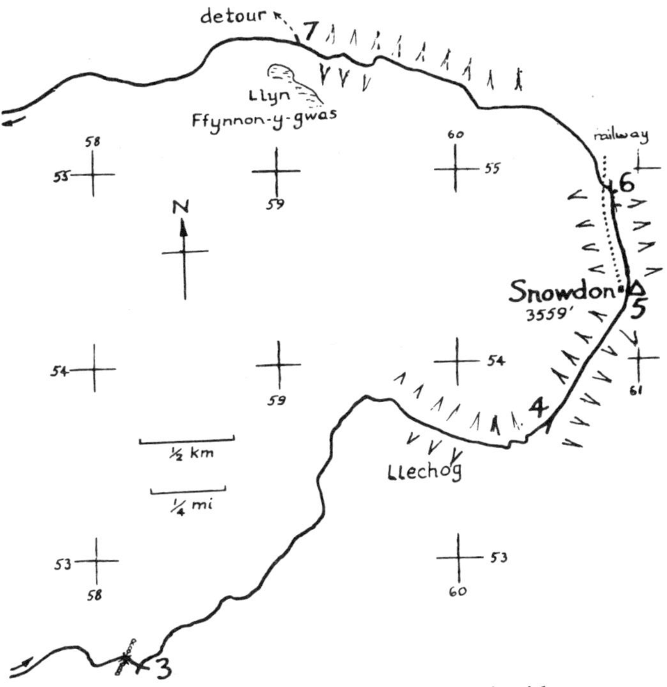

small iron gate along clear path. **4** On up main ridge to summit. **5** On down with railway on your L. **6** At second upright stone marker cross railway and take path that soon bears L down broad side ridge. **7** On near col unless you wish to make an enjoyable detour NW to Moel Cynghorion, W along its ridge and S. **8** After going through gate (with ladder stile 50 m to its L) watch for a faint grass track curving L after 100 m. Follow the pairs of pole stumps soon with a stream on your R. **9** At larger stream and fence, go ½ R to gate. Through it and at once over bridge and on to cross ladder stile. Then turn R down for 50 m and bear L over field, not far from its bottom wall, to far corner. **10** Here through gate, next gate, and two gates. **11** Near farm, go through gate and bear R down track. Just after last building, go through gate and at once L through gate and over stream. Cross field and over bridge. **12** R along track. **13** L along road.

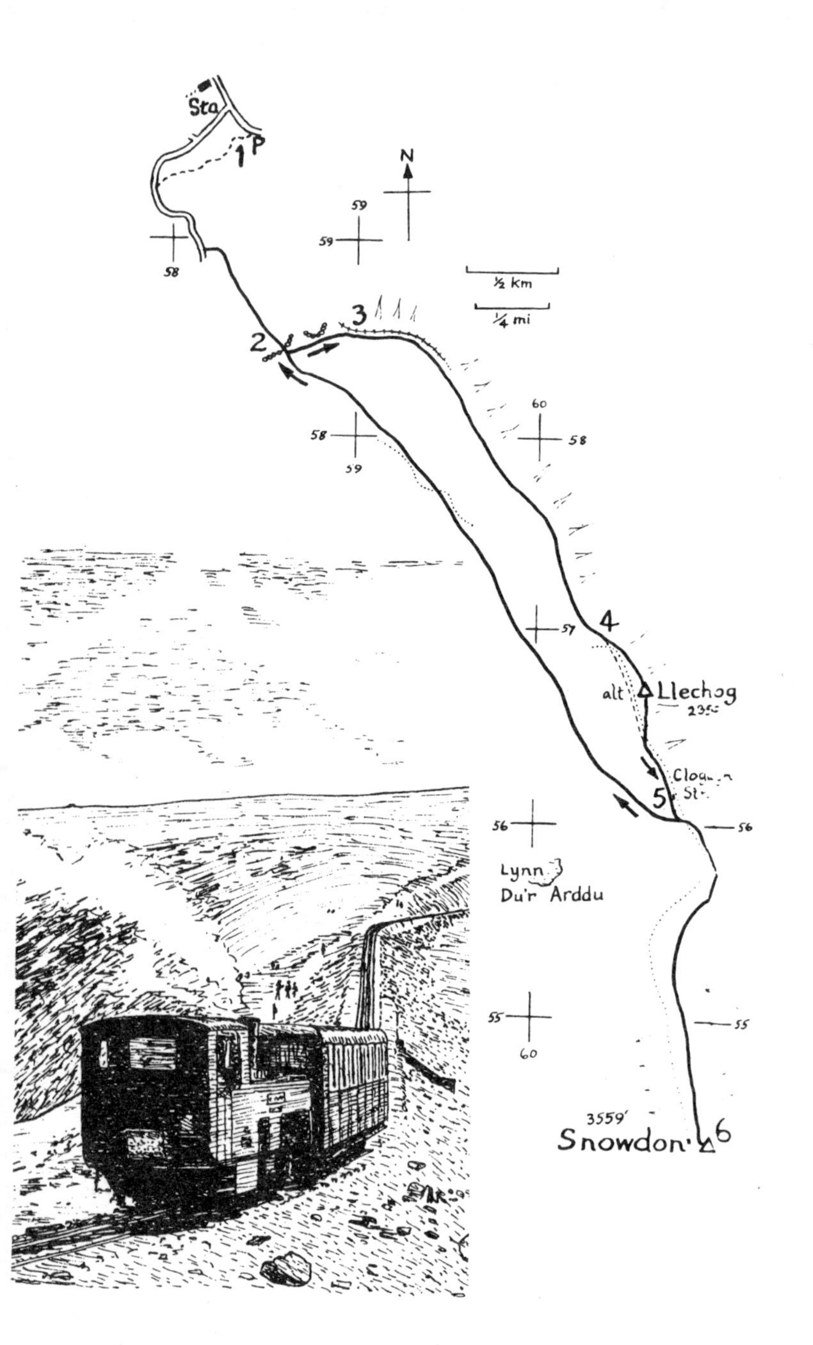

Sta
1 P
N
58
59
59
½ km
¼ mi
2
3
60
58
58
59
4
57
alt
Llechog
5
56
56
Lynn
Du'r Arddu
55
55
60
3559'
Snowdon
6

21 SNOWDON FROM LLANBERIS

(14.5 km, 9 mi, 3200 ft) Map 115, S

Summary. The ascent up a ridge has impressive views down to the Llanberis Pass and spectacular ones in all directions in the final stages. The descent is by the usual route on the side of the ridge. An easy walk, though the return path is rough in places.
Park near footpath sign near Victoria Hotel (584 595) 400 m SE of station.

1 Go along track (it later narrows). Turn L up road and L up path at signpost. **2** Through gate in wall and L up easy grass (no path) soon passing R of various walls to crest of ridge. **3** Follow fence up ridge. **4** A rocky section can be avoided by keeping just R of railway. **5** Walk R of railway to join main path soon after Clogwyn station. **6** Return from summit down main path. (Or for a change walk L of railway and join main path when railway reaches it again 300 m before Clogwyn Station.)

Llyn Llydaw from Snowdon.

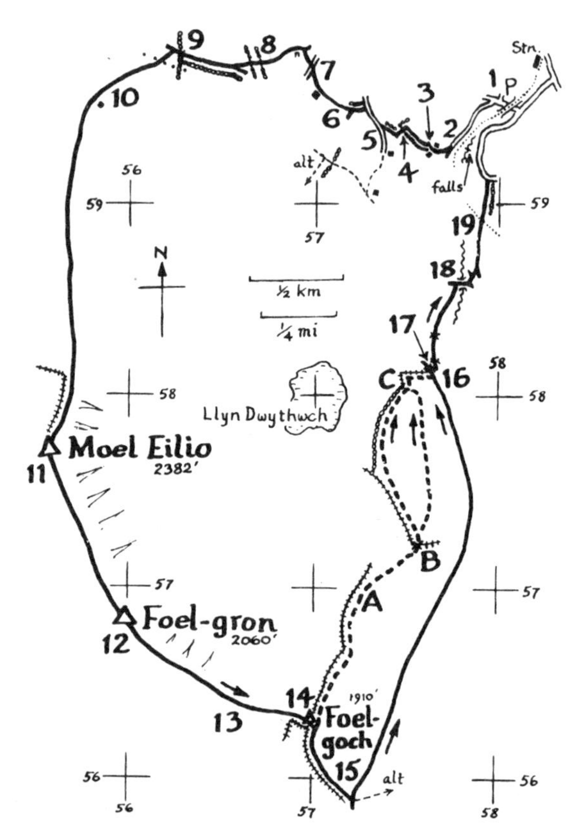

22 MOEL EILIO

(11.5 km, 7¼ mi, 2400 ft) Map 115, S

Summary. After a gentle ascent of Moel Eilio with its ancient cairn, there is a splendid ridge walk with fine views of Llyn Cwellyn, Anglesey and many mountain ranges including Snowdon. The return is easy after a short fairly steep descent down grass. If preferred a pathless ridge of rough grass passing near Llyn Dwythwch may be used for descent. In the lowland regions you will find a spectacular waterfall. It is also possible to ascend a side ridge, which has steeper start, by going L along road (later track) at point 5; R along track until just past gate in

wall; L up ridge to stile and on.
Park in side road near railway 'bridge' (581 595) reached by going along a side turning 100 m S of Snowdon mountain railway terminus, and turning first right.

1 Go NW under bridge and soon bear L up steep minor road. **2** Just after waterfall (best seen by crossing railway at gate) fork R up track. **3** When track ends, pass just R of the last building and at once turn L along path by wall (kept on your L). **4** Path turns L through gate for 50 m, then turns R by wall (on your R). **5** On along road 150 m, then L along grassy track with wall on its R. **6** At vague fork bear R over stile beside gate. Follow grass track, passing just R of buildings. **7** At road go through gate opposite and up vague path for 80 m to reach clear path. Turn L up this soon bearing L as it passes to the R of small girder framework. **8** On through 2 iron gates, soon joining track with wall on the L. **9** Go over stile by gate in wall and half L up grass to the second pole on this side of the wall. Just past here follow a low grassy bank. **10**. It passes R of ruin and goes up the broad ridge. Later there is a fence on your R. **11** At Moel Eilio go half L down ridge near steep ground on your L. **12** After next rise carry on SE, still near steep ground on your L. **13** On up to pass L of fence corner. On to Foel-goch. ● **14** On over stile and half R down by fence (on your R) to track at col. **15** Turn L down track (or first go up next ridge to Moel Cynghorion and back). **16** When you reach a fence that goes up the side of the end of the ridge on your L, go on 30 m to stile. **17** Go R over stile along path and soon L to stile and on over field to third stile. On to bridge. **18** Over bridge and at once go L 30 m along path to fork. Here go on (along R fork) to clear path and L (N/NE) along it. **19** Over railway and on to road. Turn L down road.

22A Descent via ridge. (11 km, 7 mi, 2400 ft)
Follow walk 22 to stage 13 (Foel-goch). Here cross stile and turn L down ridge by fence on your L. **A** Leave fence and make for stile in fence corner ahead on ridge. **B** Here either go on along crest of ridge, bearing L to a wall when descent steepens at end of ridge, or follow fence (later wall) kept on your L down L side of ridge. **C** At end of wall go down 40 m by old fence and R with fence to track. Turn L 30 m and follow walk 22 stage 17.

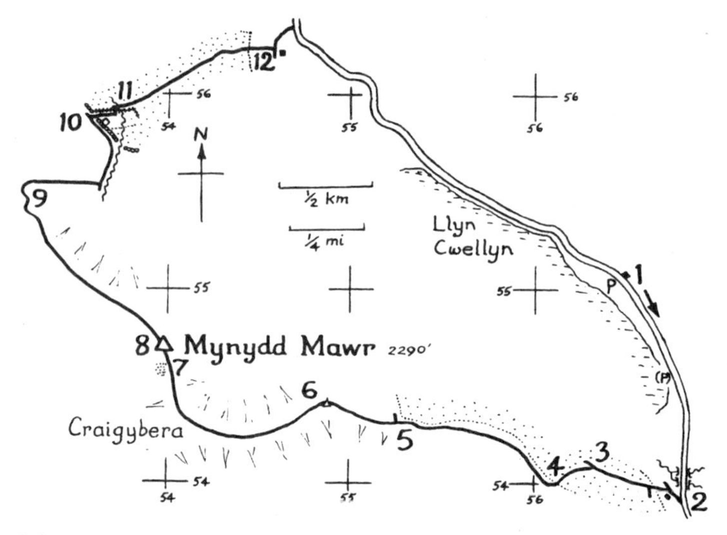

23 MYNYDD MAWR

(10 km, 6¼ mi, 1900 ft) Map 115, S

Summary. After climbing through the forest there follows a delightful ridge with views of Llyn Cwellyn and other lakes below the fine mountains of the Nantlle ridge and the Snowdon range. You also pass close to the fine crags of Craigybera. The descent starts well on heathery slopes but there is a pathless section leading to a dark wood, followed by road without pavement. One third of the walk is on road. You may prefer to return the way you came. If misty at the top, turn back.

Park at the Snowdon Ranger car park (564 550) by Llyn Cwellyn on the A4085 N of Rhyd-ddu.

1 Go SE along road. **2** Soon after crossing bridge go sharp R along track. At once, after passing house, go through gate half L up to gate at forest edge, and on. **3** At fork go L up path by poles. **4** On leaving forest go R along path near its edge. **5** On up clear path above top of forest. **6** At top of rise bear L along ridge. Move to L of path for fine crag views. **7** Near top, the cairned route passes just R of a large scree patch which might be mistaken for the summit. **8** Go on NW down gentle slopes (some scree). Cairns show the start but bring you too far to L so move away from them until there is steep ground on your right. Soon pick up a good path. **9** At mine hole leave path and bear R along the bottom of the slope. Go roughly E and turn L along path beside stream, then by wall. **10** Turn R through small iron gate just past folds. On (E) along forest edge. Over stile by stream and along by fence (now on your R) past second stile. **11** On into forest at first gently up. **12** Down field past footpath sign to building. Here L along track. R along road.

From Craigybera looking to Llyn Nantlle Uchaf.

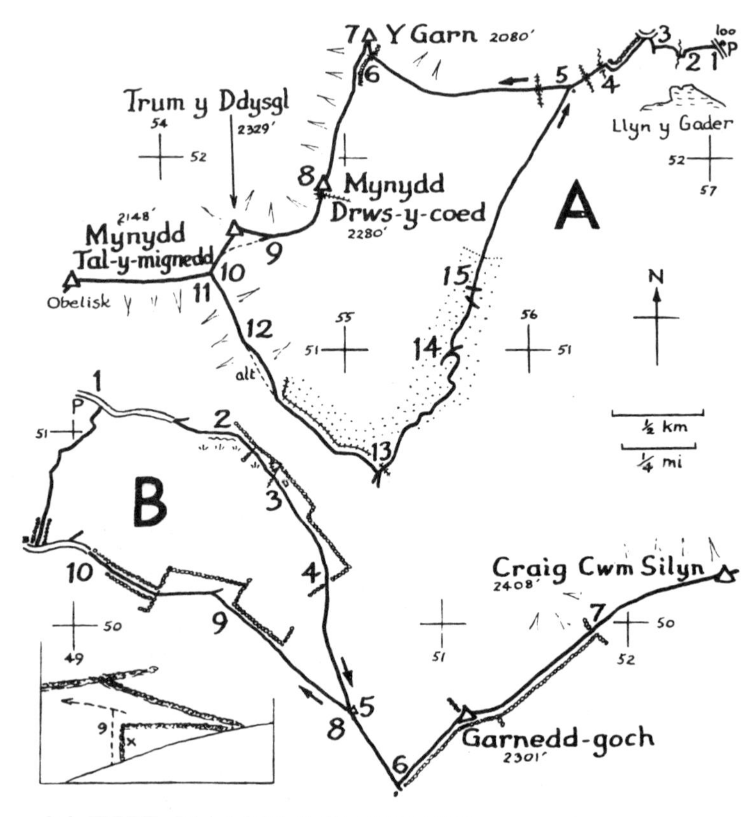

24 THE NANTLLE RIDGE

Map 115,S

Summary. I have divided this splendid ridge into 2, but the whole ridge can be walked from Rhyd-ddu if you can meet a car at the other end. The hardest part is just S of Y Garn, where there is some scrambling. Paths are slightly vague below the SW end of the ridge. Wet patches are crossed after leaving forest on the return to Rhyd-ddu or near start of walk B.

Park just S of Rhyd-ddu (571 526) or for walk 24 B: 1.5 mi (2 km) W from Nantlle village on the B4418 turn L along road towards Llanllyfni. After 1.0 mi (1.6 km) turn L along road for 1.0 mi to a small parking area. (491 512).

To walk the whole ridge (12.5 km, 7¾ mi, 3100 ft) follow walk 24A to the Obelisk (stage 10) and bear L (S then SW) along ridge to walk 24B point 6. Here turn R and follow stages 8 to 10.

24A North East Section (10.5 km, 6½ mi, 2400 ft)

1 Cross road and go down path opposite loo. **2** Turn L by stream and soon R over bridge and R over track on path marked by arrows. It joins a track to reach gate at road. **3** Here turn sharp L along path with wall by your R. **4** By gate go L over bridge and on to stile 150 m ahead. **5** 80 m past stile go one third R at large boulder marked 'ridge'. Aim for craggy end of ridge and stile. (Follow arrows.) Over stile and on up path towards top. **6** Over stile and half R to Y Garn. **7** Turn S along ridge. Soon some scrambling. (You can keep away from steep drop on R by bearing L up boulders.) **8** On over summit and stile. **9** When path becomes level leave it and go half R up grass to regain ridge crest. **10** After nearly level section bear half R (E) down and up to obelisk. ● Turn back to point 10. **11** Go R down a side ridge. **12** Path goes L of slight rise, or you can stay on crest. **13** Go L through gate. **14** When stony track reaches forest road go R along it 50 m and L along road. **15** Go L over bridge and at once R along path, then track leading out of forest.

24B South West Section (11 km, 7 mi, 1800 ft)

1 Go up road, through gate and on over pathless grass roughly towards distant fold near a wall. Keep L of marsh, soon joining path by ditch. **2** Through gate and over wettish ground to cross over wooden bars just R of fence. **3** Pass just R of fold. **4** Cross wall at stone post 100 m from end of wall. Go up clear path at 30° to wall. **5** Where path is vague go towards dip in skyline. Follow stone posts. Later aim S/SE to wall gap. **6** Go L by wall kept on your R. **7** On to cairn 2408 ft. Return same way to point 5. **8** Watch for cairn marking path junction and take vague path down easy slope NW to walk by wall X in drawing. **9** When wall turns R keep on to join track to road. **10** On along road and R along track between walls just before house.

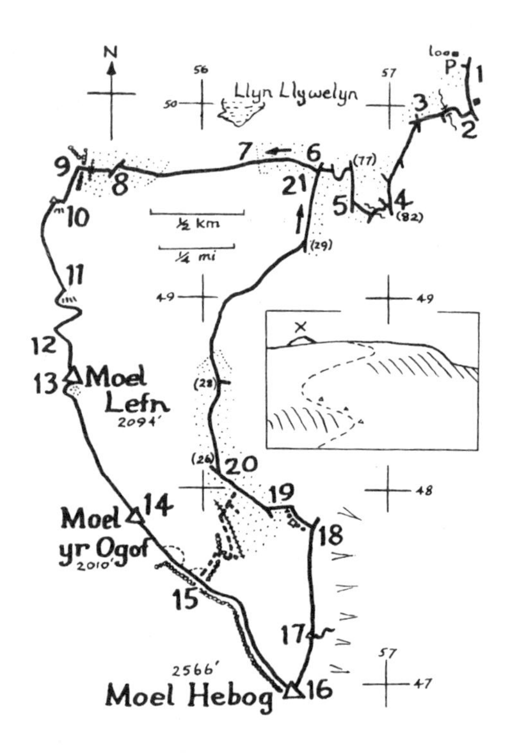

25 THE MOEL HEBOG RIDGE

(12 km, 7¼ mi, 2800 ft) Map 115, S,H

Summary. After a maze of forest paths (with views at times) there is an attractive open path (which may have a wet patch) and a further wooded stretch before the very pleasant and easy ridge is reached. Then a short descent down a rocky ridge gets you back to the forest, where there are still some long open sections, partly due to felling of some areas. In the forest, junctions are often numbered. (No numbers seen 1993.) These are put in brackets in the following notes and map. Avoid the ridges in mist as their paths are not clear cut. (Use the short cut to get off Moel Hebog.)

Park in Beddgelert Forest Car Park (574 502). Entrance 3.5 km (2 mi) N of village.

1 Turn R out of parking area down forest road. **2** Turn R 50 m after house on L. Over bridge and on. **3** Go half L at junction. **4** After passing first track on R go R up track at junction (82). Ignore track off R to gate and named house. 20 m after crossing stream go R up path near wood edge. **5** At track go R 200 m to junction (77) and L up track. **6** Just after it bends sharply L, go R up small path. Soon L along road and at once R along path (Blue markers). **7** On along path in open then back in forest. **8** At road go L 80 m then R up path to wood edge. **9** Here over stile and wall. Turn L along by wall (on your L). **10** Over 'stile', R 15 m to cairn and half L up small grass path passing quarry (on your L). Keep on if path fades. Soon first summit is seen. Aim for X (see drawing) over easy ground (no path). **11** Avoid large rock-face by bearing R then L up cairned path. Then follow path bearing R (with steep ground on its R). **12** At level ground go L to the L of the rocky knolls and then R to the cairn (Moel Lefn). **13** On to Moel yr Ogof. (Avoid boulder patch by a detour to R.) **14** On along ridge with cairns down steep rough section. (Or avoid this by short detour L on grass.) Follow wall (on your R) down to col. The boggy patch is avoided by easy scrambles. The final steep rough section can again be avoided by a detour L. **15** Over old wall and on up to Moel Hebog by wall on your R. **16** Turn L down ridge with steep ground on your R. **17** Ground steepens at cairn marking start of descent to Beddgelert. Ignore this rough path and keep on down rocky/grassy ridge with steep ground near your R. (Path and cairns here and there.) **18** At col follow old wall L down off ridge. Soon after passing folds (on your L) go L through gate into forest. **19** Half R down forest road. **20** Fork R at junction (26). **21** Here return the way you came. (R at junction (77) for 200 m. L down path. L along track. L along main track etc.)

Short cut: 15 At col go L by wall (on your R). Go R through wall gap (now with wall on your L) for 30 m. Then cross wall and go down grass towards forest. (Can be wet patches.) Follow fence L to stile. R down path in forest. Over one road and L along the next. Follow stage 20.

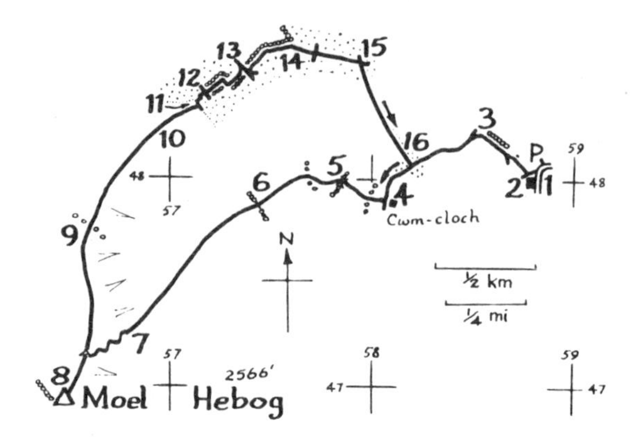

26 MOEL HEBOG FROM BEDDGELERT

(8 km, 5 mi, 2400 ft) Map 115, S,H

Summary. This short walk climbs an easy grassy ridge but has a steep rough section a little before the summit. Descent is down a good rocky ridge that leads to paths through the forest. The flat section after Cwm-cloch can be rather wet. If there is mist at the top it is better to return the way you came.

Park in car park off A498 at W end of Beddgelert (588 481).

1 Leave car park and go R along road and on up drive passing Royal Goat Hotel (on your L). **2** At signpost go R through gate and on over grass to large concrete 'block'. Here go through gate and along track with wall on your R. **3** The track turns L and joins farm drive. On up this through belt of pines. **4** At Cwm-cloch farm turn R over stile and cross field through wall gap to second stile. **5** Here go half L up cairned path which bears R just before next wall. Over wall and on up grassy path to ridge. At ridge go L up it. (Cairns.) **6** On through gate in wall. **7** Up rough winding path to large cairn and L to summit. **8** Back to large cairn, but ignore rough path and keep on down rocky/grassy ridge with steep ground near your R. (Path and cairns here and there.) **9** At col crossed by old wall carry on along ridge which bears slightly R. Keep R of the now broad ridge. (Faint path in places.) **10** At the ridge end go on more steeply down to forest edge. L along edge gently down to corner of forest. **11** Here R over low fence, L over low wall and R a few m down to forest track. **12** On down path between walls, R 50 m by wall and then L down by wall (on your R) to forest track. **13** Go R 50 m along track then L down path with wall on your L. Later wall and path turns half R. **14** At final corner of field on your L go ½ R along path, soon crossing forest track. **15** At next iron swing gate turn R along track. **16** Go L down the drive you came up.

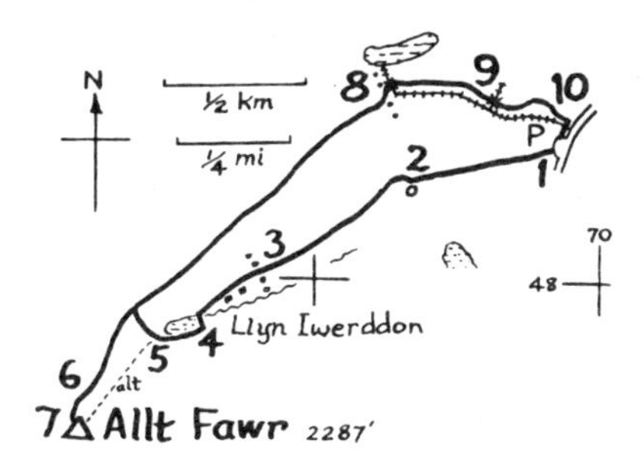

27 ALLT FAWR

(5 km, 3 mi, 1100 ft) Map 115, CV,H

Summary. An easy walk in very pleasant country made attractive by many small lakes. Having reached the top it is well worth exploring the area to the W. before the return along a ridge. Do not go past Llyn Iwerddon if it is misty as paths are not clear. Maybe a few wet patches, but largely dry.

Park in layby 150 m S of top of Crimea Pass (699 485) N of Blaenau Ffestiniog.

1 Go W along grassy track to air shaft. **2** Here go half R up small path that soon bears L and fades. Keep on (SW) up valley keeping just R of wettish area. **3** As route levels cross old wall, pass 2 ruins and reach the R end of dam. **4** Cross dam and turn R beside lake and over a second dam. **5** 50 m past lake go R up to col and L along path on ridge. (Or reach top directly by going one third L up grass and rocks.) **6** When gradient eases make for summit. **7** Return to col, then on along ridge path. **8** At line of poles bear L to cross stile in fence. On by fence (on your R). **9** Over stile and on by fence. When it steepens, move 20 m from fence to easier slope. **10** Just before road go R through gate.

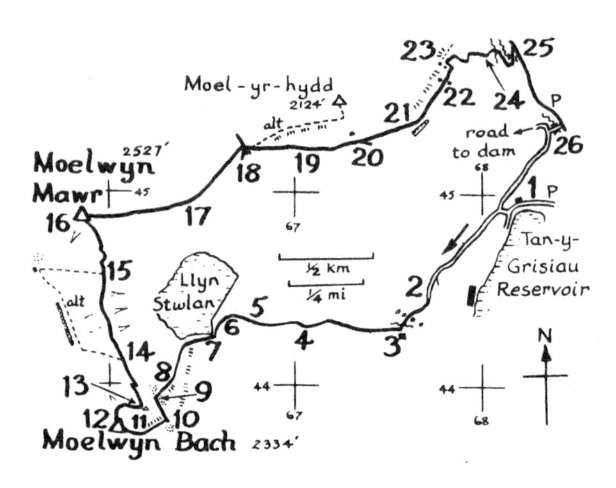

28 MOELWYN BACH AND MAWR FROM THE EAST

(9 km, 5¾ mi, 2500 ft) Map 115, 124, H

1 Walk W past centre. Ignore first L fork to power station. Go up next L fork. **2** At road end go over gate and on in same direction as road along path. Soon it bears R, then L, through old wall and over stream to a pillar. **3** Here turn R up old tramway. **4** At next 2 pillars path is level before a steepish stone-lined incline. **5** On to L end of dam. **6** Here go L up short rough section and across level ground to far end of small dam. **7** Here follow path running about 40 m from lake edge. At fenced enclosure bear L along base of a line of outcrops, towards Moelwyn Bach. **8** When near a separate outcrop to the R cross over to it and go across valley (no path) to use a grass strip to get to top of slate heaps. **9** Here turn L along rough path. After a triangular hole on your R, ignore steps and go on nearly level path over scree. **10** When path is no longer banked by stones on the L and there is a slate heap 50 m ahead, turn R up grass to pass R of heap and follow up lower edge of large outcrop. **11** At nearly level ground beyond outcrop, bear R (NW) aiming slightly L of what seems the highest point. Soon reach summit. **12** Here go N/NE towards Moelwyn Mawr to a small pool, beyond which is a severe drop and fine view. At pool turn R with steep ground on L. After 150 m cairn is reached after a slight descent. **13** Here turn L down path. Go carefully down a short scree zig-zag the rest is quite easy. **14** At col go on up. The first scramble is probably the hardest. (To avoid this ridge go half L down path from col. Soon turn two thirds R along gently rising path by wall. At spoil heap by ruins turn R up easy grass to rejoin ridge.) **15** At small col on up winding path. As gradient eases bear L to Moelwyn Mawr. **16** Turn sharp R (E) down broad ridge. **17** Bear to L along a smaller ridge that goes towards Moel-yr-hydd. Later follow slight path just L of outcrops on this ridge. **18** When a path joins from the L at cairn, go by the L of outcrop just behind cairn to clear path descending E. (To reach Moel-yr-hydd soon go half L off this path to outcrops and follow them up (on their crest or just L of them) until path is level. Then go L to top. Return the same way.) **19** When path becomes vague go on down a short distance to a peaty area. A path goes just L of this and then crosses a much larger wet area. (If too wet detour round to the L.) **20** At fork with tunnel on your L go on (not half R). Where path is vague keep on. Aim for the small lake ahead. **21** Pass lake (on your R) along path. Pass by old buildings keeping near outcrops on your L. **22** Go between 2 pillars and down steep slaty incline to flat area with more buildings. Here go L along the edge of this area to 2 more pillars (20 m before reaching outcrops and level grass path). Here go R down second incline. **23** On down rough path that bears R then L. It becomes a smoother clear stony winding path in grass. **24** 50 m before stream it bears R to cross small slate bridge. Here go R along raised path. Turn L to the first large bridge and go L across it and on to wide track. **25** Here sharp R along track. **26** Turn R along road over bridge. Soon go L down road.

Summary. The first section climbs gently above Tan-y-Grisiau Reservoir, to reach Llyn Stwlan. Not long after crossing the dam Moelwyn Bach is reached. The splendid rocky ridge running up to Moelwyn Mawr has some easy scrambles, but can be avoided. An easy descent follows, with a worthwhile visit to Moel-yr-hydd as an optional extra. The final steep descent uses paths and inclines of old quarries, and passes fine waterfalls. The railway obstructs the direct public path to the dam; my route is a practical alternative to use until a new right of way is agreed upon. Of course the road to the dam can be used instead. Paths are often

vague and there are wet patches in stages 19, 20. Do not attempt the walk if it is misty.
Park near the CEGB visitors' centre (683 449) Tan-y-grisiau, SW of Blaenau Ffestiniog.

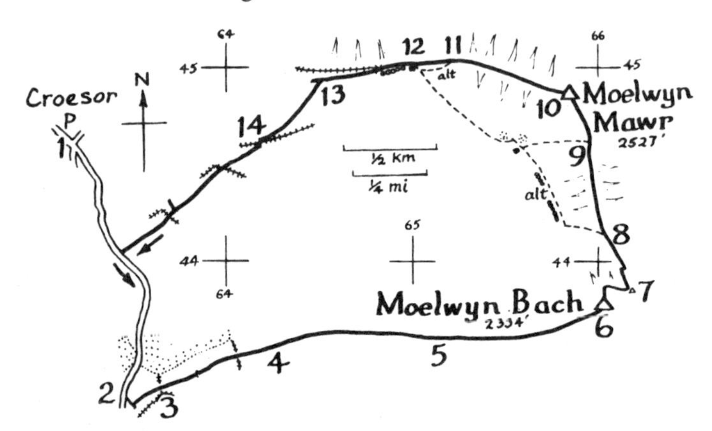

29 MOELWYN BACH AND MAWR FROM CROESOR

(9 km, 5¾ mi, 2400 ft) Map 115, 124, H

Summary. After starting up a scenic minor road there is a broad and gentle ridge leading to Moelwyn Bach. Moelwyn Mawr is then reached by a fine rocky scramble which can be avoided if desired. Another pleasant ridge is used for the final descent. There may be wet patches near stage 3.

Park at Croesor (631 447) reached along 3 km (2 mi) narrow, but not steep, road.

1 Turn L out of car park and go on over cross-road. **2** 200 m past plantation fork half L along track for 30 m, then go L up vague path (before reaching fence). **3** Through fence gap and on through gates (all 100 m R of plantation). **4** On (E) up easy grass towards highest point on ridge. (Path not always clear.) **5** When gradient eases follow path seen ahead in grass R of outcrops. **6** At summit go L (N/NE) towards Moelwyn Mawr to a small pool, beyond which is a severe drop and fine view. At pool turn R with

steep ground on L. After 150 m a cairn is reached after a slight descent. **7** Here turn L down path. Go carefully down short scree zig-zag; the rest is quite easy. **8** At col go on up! The first scramble is probably the hardest. (To avoid this ridge go half L down path from col. Soon turn two-thirds R along gently rising path by wall. ● At spoil heap by ruins turn R up easy grass to rejoin ridge.) **9** At small col go on up winding path. As gradient eases bear L to Moelwyn Mawr. **10** Turn W/NW down grassy ridge. **11** After a slight rise a brief scramble down follows. (To avoid it bear L down grass at the dip, regaining the crest of the ridge at a 'tower'.) **12** At 'tower' take path on R of wall. Over stile and down ridge with fence on your R. **13** When fence goes down R side of ridge, turn half L off ridge. Soon reach and follow fence on your L. **14** Through gate and W/SW to and through second gate. Follow track to road, ignoring track going off R.
To bypass Moelwyn Mawr follow walk to stage 8. Here follow instructions in brackets as far as large spoil heap. Just before heap turn L down grass to join path passing several ruins. It then goes down to join a level tramway taking you to a 'tower'. There follow stage 12 etc.

Moelwyn Bach seen from Moelwyn Mawr.

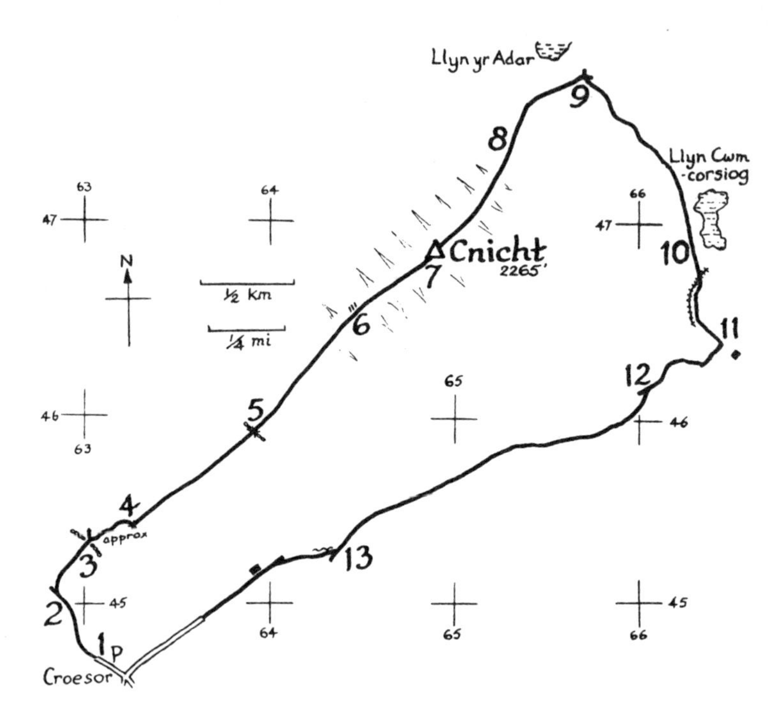

30 CNICHT

(10.5 km, 6½ mi, 1800 ft) Map 115, 124, H

Summary. The start is reached after driving 3.5 km (2 mi) along a narrow gently rising and fairly straight road. After a short climb there is a long splendid ridge with one easy scramble near the summit. Several lakes are passed or seen on the next section, where there may be some wet patches. After reaching a quarry the descent begins along a path (rough at first) down the side of a ridge back to Croesor. Here there are fine views, streams and waterfalls. Not long after crossing the summit, the ridge and path is less clear, so if mist appeared it would be better to turn back.
Park at Croesor car park (631 447).

1 Turn R out of car park and go NW up road, then track among trees. **2** At the top in the open fork half R along track. 3 At wall and stile go one third R up grass path towards the conical peak of

Cnicht. Soon, at a heap of slate, go one third R over stream and up clear grass track. 50 m before fold go R along path through rushes and up to wall stile. **4** Here over stile and L up path on ridge. **5** Over stile and along level path on scree. **6** Not far from top there is an easy scramble just on the R of a sloping rocky outcrop. **7** At top keep on along ridge. When it widens keep nearer the L edge to make sure you don't go down a side ridge forking half R. **8** When Llyn yr Adar is seen ahead make for the rocky mini-ridge 150 m to its R. **9** 50 m beyond the shallow col turn R down cairned path. It winds, keeping roughly at the same height. **10** By Llyn Cwm-corsiog the path fades over wettish ground. Follow cairns S/SE over old fence. Follow fence (20 m to your R) down a clearer path. At bottom of slope path goes half L towards mine buildings. **11** On reaching the flat slaty area, go R along a slaty track to the R hand end of this area. Here a clear track goes towards Cnicht and then bears L. **12** Soon fork L down path which runs along hillside. **13** At fork go half R down towards buildings, at first with stream on your R. **14** On along track, then road.

Cnicht as seen from Allt Fawr.

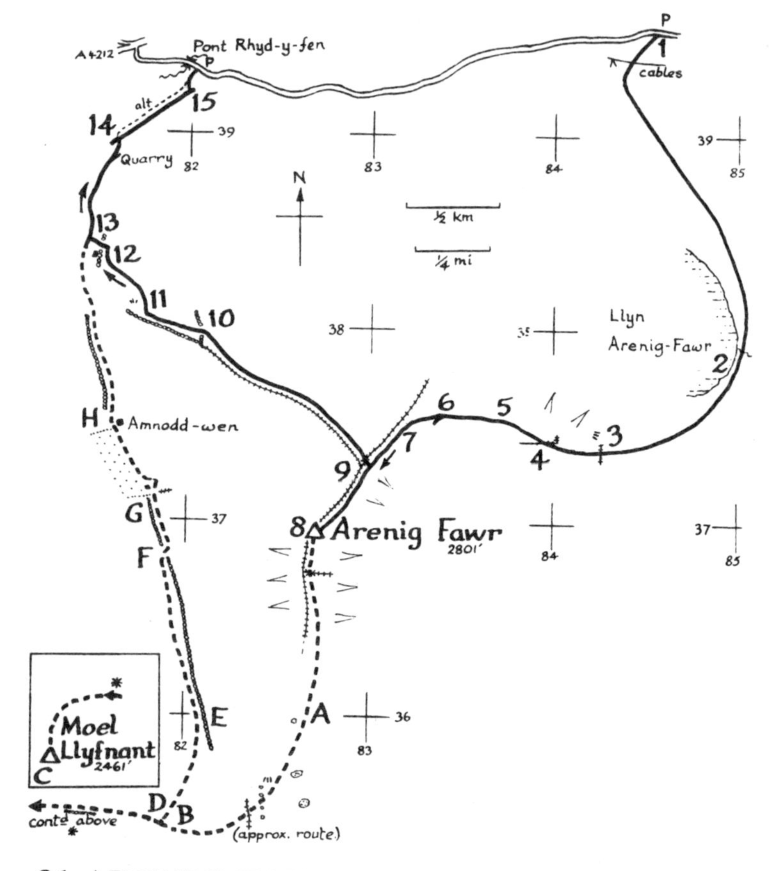

31 ARENIG FAWR

(11 km, 7 mi, 2000 ft) Map 124, B

1 Go along track, soon passing under cables. **2** Cross dam and stream. (If full, crossing is easier a little downstream.) On along clear path up a grassy ridge that bears R round the lake. **3** On over old fence with outcrop 30 m to R. **4** When ground levels cross next fence by stone steps 30 m after fence is met. Soon path goes NW over nearly level grass. **5** Path turns half L as ground starts to rise. **6** At a large bare patch where path bears half L along the side of the ridge, leave path and go on up grass to top of ridge keeping R of scree. **7** Here bear L along ridge to summit with a fence on your R all the way. ● **8** Turn back the way you came. **9** At fence junction turn L over stile and go down by fence (electric) on your L. The ridge and path slowly bear L for some time. **10** Cross old wall 30 m to R of the wall/fence you have been following. On down small grass path. **11** The path fades after about 250 m. Turn R to skirt rushy patches, then bear L to make for a small rocky knoll, with a length of wall in view just on its L. **12** Go R by the wall a short distance down to ruin. Here L over field to track and fence. **13** R along track. **14** After quarry join old railway track. (Here path should cross railway and run beside it, but it may be easier to stay on the railway and leave it through holes in old fence when near pylon.) **15** Cross grass to gate on R of bridge. Go R along road.

31A Arenig Fawr and Moel Llyfnant (16.5 km, 10¼ mi, 2700 ft)
Follow walk 31 to Arenig Fawr. **8** Carry on down ridge. Loose scree can be avoided to the L. **A** Follow path passing just L of pools, then by old wall for a while and R of 4 larger pools. Then it soon bears R round outcrop (on your R) to cross old wall. The col you will reach is seen ahead (W). When path fades go down rough grass to col. There should be a stile to cross the single-wire electric fence. If not, crawl under it. **B** Cross col by path and go up, at first by old wall, bearing L to Moel Llyfnant. **C** Return to col. **D** Bear L along one of the nearly level sheep paths, aiming to reach the long wall that goes to the plantation. **E** At ravine a path carries on L of wall and most of the nearby trees. It disappears among boulders and across wet patches. **F** 300 m before plantation take the clear track on R of wall. **G** Through fence gap just R of ruin at plantation corner. **H** After ruin (Amnodd-wen) track bears R with wall on its L. Now follow walk 31 stage 14.

Summary. A stony track leads to Llyn Arenig-Fawr, backed by impressive crags and steep ground. After a short fairly steep section the rocky summit is reached by a gently climbing path. The return is also easy, ending along the minor road. The view includes many of the ranges of Snowdonia and heather is a further attraction. Paths are mostly clear and dry while the few vague wettish sections should not be hard to follow. The fence is a useful guide down if caught by mist. The main interest in the

extension to Moel Llyfnant is the descent of the pleasant ridge S from Arenig Fawr with many pools and outcrops. Later there are pathless and wettish sections.
Park in the limited space (846 395) 3 km (2 mi) E from where the minor road leaves the A4212. This is at the top of a rise where a track turns SW off road and Llyn Celyn is below to the NE. (Or park near Pont Rhyd-y-fen and walk along road first.)

32 ARENIG FACH

(3.5 km, 2¼ mi, 1100 ft) Map 124, B
Park by the A4212 near drive to Rhyd-y-fen (826 400) and go N through gate opposite drive. Aim for gap in highest wall seen. There go on up through heather. Return the same way. No path.

33 THE ARAN RIDGE

Map 124, B, CI
Summary. This long easy ridge with many rocky outcrops is best done as a non-circular walk if you can arrange transport. There may be a wet area to cross at the S end before you slant down the side of a fine steep-sided valley. A visit to the S end can now be made circular, but only by using a path with several wet patches and little to commend it other than the impressive ravine near the start (and the remains of an aircraft engine further on). The S end has very good views.
Park at bend in the B4403 road (880 297) SE of Llanuwchllyn, or for walk 33B near the end of the Cwm Cywarch road (854 185).

To walk the whole ridge (14 km, 8¾ mi, 2700 ft) follow walk 33A and carry on S along ridge over Erw y Ddafad-ddu (2830 ft) to Aran Fawddwy, which towers above Craiglyn Dyfi. Here follow walk 33B stage 10. Do not go on past Aran Benllyn in mist.

33A Aran Benllyn (11.5 km, 7¼ mi, 2400 ft)
1 Go SW along track at bend in road. **2** At top of rise go half R along grassy track over stile. **3** After passing outcrops on your L fork L along path (S) towards the ridge. Later there is a fence on your R. **4** White arrows mark a short detour to avoid a steep rocky section. **5** Path bears L to (or close to) crest of ridge. Later

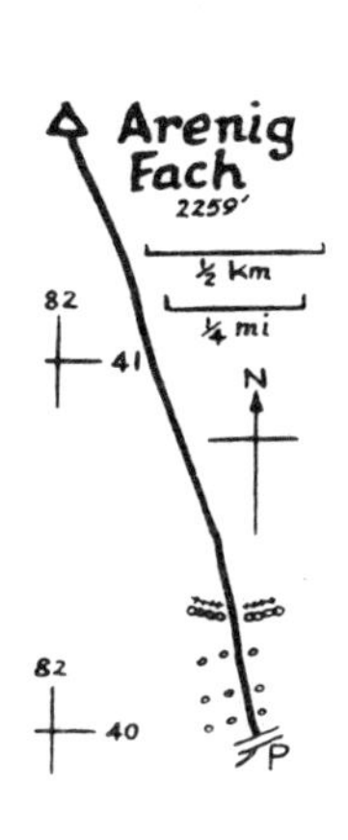

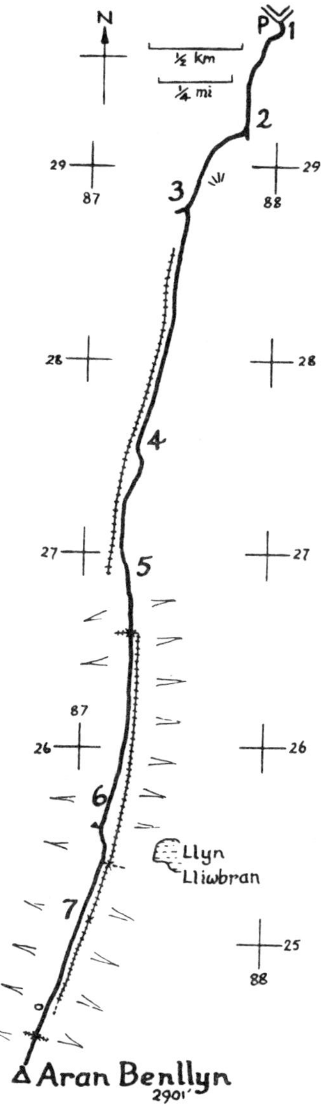

over stile and on by fence on your L. **6** At cairn at base of steep section go half L up to fence and on by it. (After this rise go L over stile and back again for a view of Llyn Lliwbran.) **7** Ignore next stile on your L. On over next stile to Aran Benllyn. Return the same way.

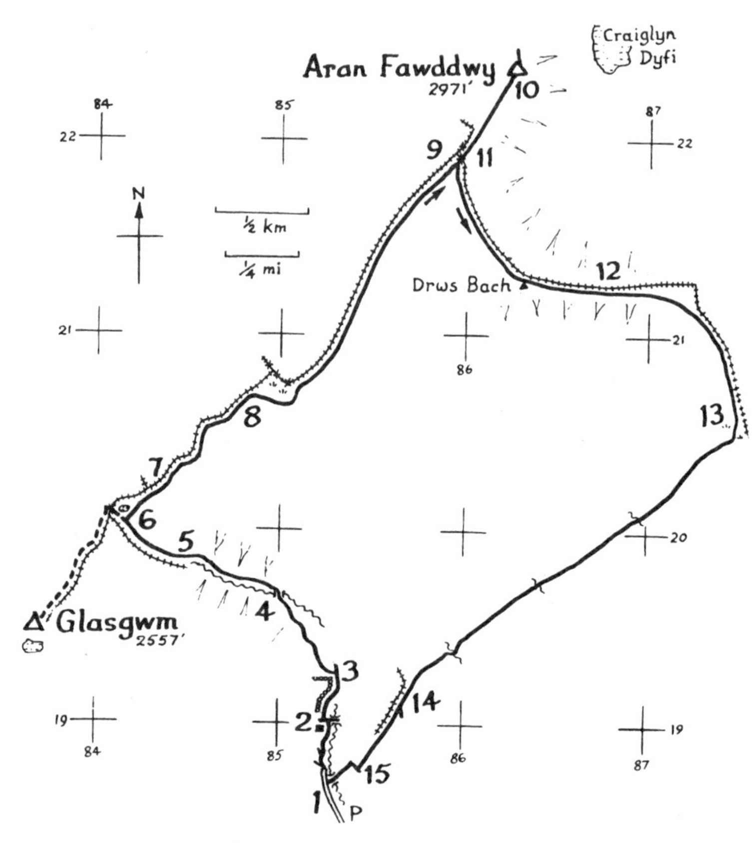

33B Aran Fawddwy (12 km, 7½ mi, 2500 ft)

1 Go on along road, ignoring farm drives on the L. **2** At bridge go L and very soon R along track with wall or fence on your L. **3** When wall turn L, leave track and bear L up wide grass path that soon bears R and winds up hill. **4** Cross bridge and go up on R of stream. The path is not always clear. White arrows help. It is never far from the stream, but near the rocky ravine it does turn away R for a while along a rough path. **5** As gradient eases there is a fence on your L to follow. **6** 100 m before stile ahead you have a choice. If you wish to climb Glasgwm, which has no right of way, cross stile and turn L up by fence. Come back the same way. (This adds 2 km, 1¼ mi, 700 ft to the walk.) Otherwise turn R 100 m before stile is reached. This route (over wet ground) is marked by yellow arrows. **7** Follow path by fence on your L. **8** A wide detour R may be needed near this wet fence junction with 3 stiles. **9** Over stile at next fence junction with 2 stiles and on up ridge to Aran Fawddwy. **10** Go SW along cairned path on ridge, later with fence on your R. **11** Cross the L of 2 stiles and turn L to walk by fence. **12** After large cairn the path leaves fence for a while. **13** At large flat area leave fence and cross wet patch to go along clear path slanting R down hillside. **14** Stay by fence when path forks. **15** When between 2 old tree-lined walls the track turns R then L down to road.

Looking South from Drws Bach.

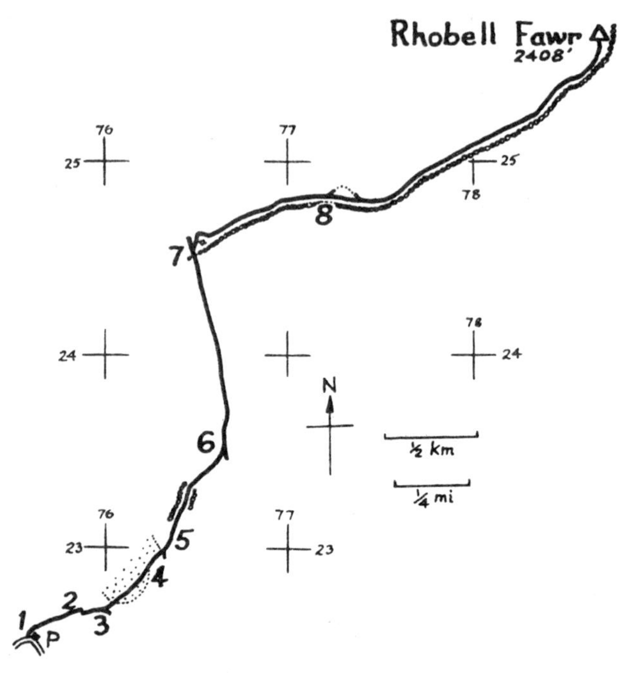

34 RHOBELL FAWR

(10½ km, 6½ mi, 1900 ft) Map 124, CI

Summary. An easy walk in pleasant country reaching a large area of heather near the col before the final rise over grass with attractive outcrops. You return the same way, as going on brings you to a wall with no gaps or stile.

Park in Llanfachreth near the school (756 225)

1 Go along track just L of school. **2** Near house go R 3m and L along track. **3** Soon, at signpost, go on along track to next sign post and gate, where you enter wood. **4** On out of wood (with wood on your L) and through gate. **5** Keep on (N/NE) as track becomes faint, soon with wall on your L and then walls on both sides. **6** Turn half L up track. **7** At col go through gate and half R up track past pens. It soon gets back to wall and runs beside it. **8** Track moves away from wall for a while, but you can stay by wall until close to summit.

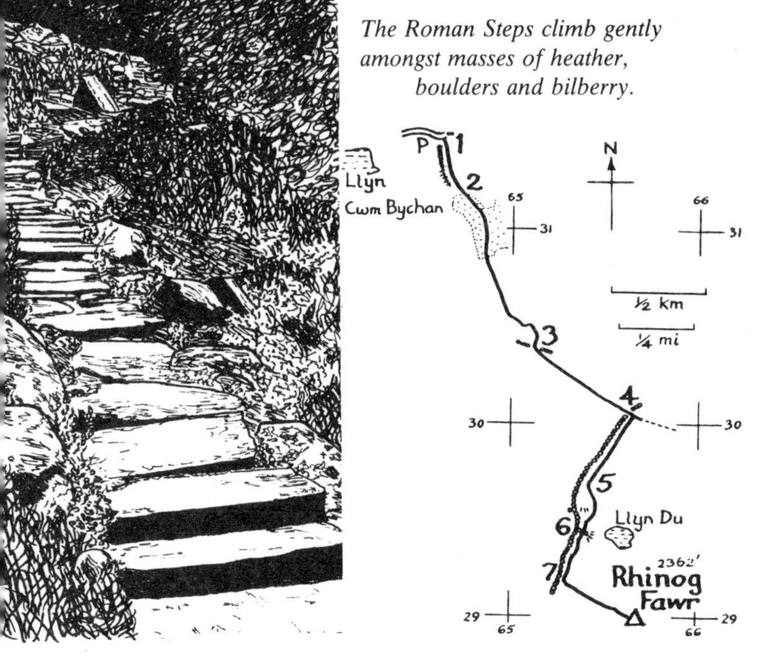

The Roman Steps climb gently amongst masses of heather, boulders and bilberry.

35 RHINOG FAWR AND THE ROMAN STEPS

(7.5 km, 4¾ mi, 1900 ft) Map 124, H

1 At the road end turn R along track. There is a wall, then fence on your R. **2** Into wood for a while. **3** After passing through wall gap path bears L along the steps. **4** At wall and nature reserve notice, turn R steeply up path near wall (on your R). **5** Path bears L away from wall to dodge large outcrop. When Llyn Du is seen, path bears R back to wall. **6** Path crosses a short low wall between outcrop and main wall. Stay near main wall until you see 3 or 4 large (1 m) boulders in the wall at the top of a slight rise. **7** Here follow path as it bears L to go up the final rise. Return the same way. On reaching point 4 it is worth going up to the top of the pass for the view before returning.

Summary. After a delightful climb through woodland, the Roman steps are reached. They are ancient, but probably

post-Roman. Parts are surprisingly well preserved and the path is hemmed in by heather and rugged mountains on both sides. Before the col a path is followed past the remote Llyn Du and up the final rise to the top. There are a few wettish patches, some easy scrambling and scree after leaving the steps. Views of several small lakes are enjoyed on this walk.
Park (not free) just past Llyn Cwm Bychan (645 314)

36 RHINOG FAWR VIA BWLCH ARDUDWY

(8 km, 5 mi, 1800 ft) Map 124, H
Summary. After a clear path with some wettish patches takes you to the col, the summit is reached by a route that is not easy to follow. Avoid it in mist or if you don't enjoy vague routes. (However, if lost, there do not seem to be any difficulties that would stop you getting to the top by choosing your own route in clear weather.) From the top a good easy return follows, which is only vague at one short section and wet at one other.
Park (not free) at road end near Maes-y-garnedd (642 270).

1 Go NE along path with wall on your R and through iron gate. **2** Later wall is left for a while. **3** On through gate and up to col. **4** Here go L up path through square hole in wall. It goes up the side of the ridge with good views R. **5** Watch for the L U-turn and a sharp R turn up the top edge of a boulder patch to reach cairn on tall boulder. Note the highest point seen (N/NW). It has a notch at the top. It is not the summit and you will pass R of it later on. **6** At this cairn go L 20 m then R along path that skirts just to L of low flat outcrops. After 50 m it climbs a 0.6 m (2 ft) rock slab, goes R along slab and clearly up in heather to cairn and on. **7** Watch for cairn where path turns half L (NW) towards that notched top. It then bears R (cairned) over flat outcrops to boulders. **8** Here go up boulders towards notched top along vague path which becomes clearer and bears R (N). **9** Llyn Trawsfynydd is seen when path becomes level. Here bear L and follow path as it winds up the slope through boulders. **10** At top of steep section go R along path 40 m, then half L up boulders. Finally SW along clear path to summit. **11** Go half L, SW, down

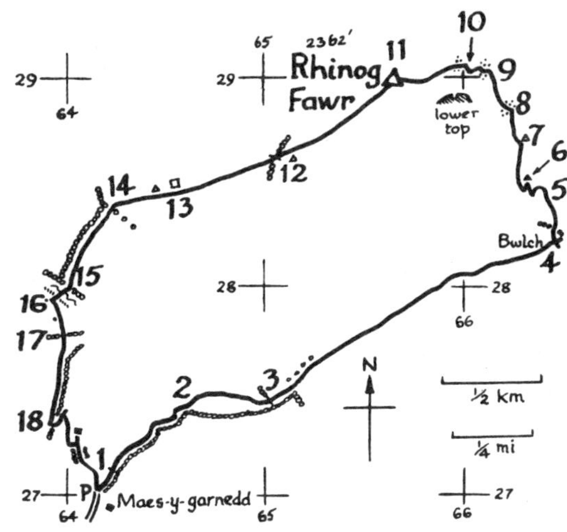

path (soon clear) towards distant cairn on a slight rise. **12** Here keep on to and over stile in wall. Follow good cairned path which seems to vanish near old folds. **13** Here carefully go on through bouldery heather past folds and on to the R end of an old wall. **14** Cross old wall and bear L down by good wall (on your R). Soon there is a path with wet patches. **15** On through wall gap and at once half R over stream and on (W/SW) to white marker post just beyond a strip of rushes. **16** At post go L (S) down grass past other posts. **17** Through iron gate and on down track which bears R and is joined by wall on its L. **18** Watch for sharp L turn through gate in wall. Follow markers leading you down grass bearing R to pass house (on your L) and at once L down through gate and R along track between 2 walls.

37 RHINOG FACH, Y LLETHR, ETC

(16 km, 10 mi, 3100 ft) Map 124, H

Summary. After a pleasant ascent along a clear track there is 400m (¼ mi) of harder route finding before Llyn Hywel is seen. The lake is very impressive from all angles, being hemmed in by steep slopes, scree and crags on three sides. The ridge is reached after passing R of the lake. A steep rough climb takes you to Rhinog Fach and back. Another climb, with a choice of routes, brings you to Y Llethr and the gentler mainly grassy part of the ridge. Beyond Diffwys, the final peak, the ridge is left using an old coach road. It crosses Pont-Scethin, a lovely old bridge.

(continued on p.86)

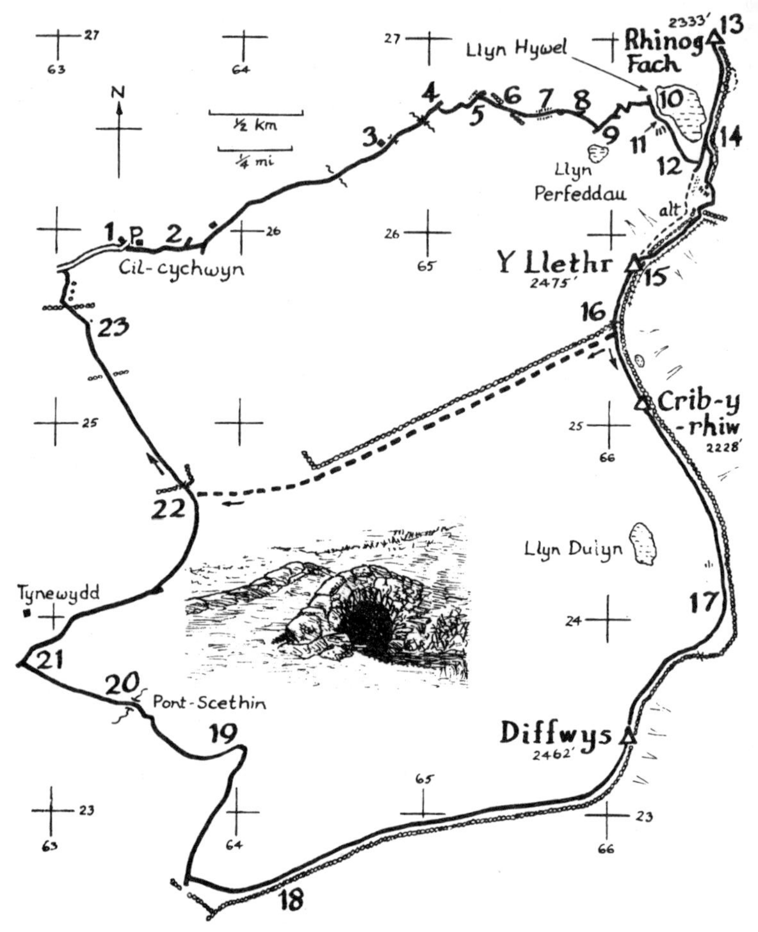

1 Go E along the track that leaves the road just R of a building. **2** Ignore track that forks down L. Soon ignore track going sharp R. **3** At ruin go on through gate and along open track. The track rises gently, then falls to a small stone slab bridge. **4** 100 m after bridge, when at the top of a second rise, turn R (S/SE) along a track that soon bears L and winds on. **5** After track has become banked on the L and is 50 m from top of rise turn half R up cairned path in heather. **6** On through wall gap E/SE along clear path making an angle of 30° with wall. Path is vague when it crosses 2 marshy places. **7** Along raised embankment and on until clear path ends at a small wet patch. Here go up a short easy scree slope to cairn at its top and bear L (SE) along path in heather. **8** On reaching a flat area the path forks. Take the R fork. Note the slight dip (E/SE) in the low ridge. This is where you will reach, but the path first goes SE until near Llyn Perfeddau. **9** Here, at path junction, turn L towards this ridge. Ignore path turning off half R, and keep on up cairned zig-zag path to the slight dip and down to Llyn Hywel. **10** Go R by the water and up clear path on small ridge until large outcrop is reached. **11** Here go steeply down by outcrop and follow rough path that climbs keeping just above scree. (One careful step is needed where there is a drop on your L.) **12** As path levels and becomes vague bear L to reach clear path. Go L down this to wall. On by wall to Rhinog Fach. (At the steep bouldery section you may like to cross wall to small steep path that skirts the rocks.) **13** Turn back to the col. **14** Here you have a choice of routes. The tougher one follows the wall (avoiding scree where possible) to its end. There cross wall and go up with outcrop on your R. At wall go up to wall junction and on between fence and wall. Through wall gap to summit. An easier route uses the 'clear path' of stage 12. It climbs just R of small outcrops and scree. When gradient eases path bears L to ridge. There go by wall to summit. **15** On down by wall on your L and over stile at wall junction. ● **16** On by wall on your L. **17** After passing above marsh path bears away from wall for a while. Then there is a rocky section up to Diffwys and on. **18** Follow wall that goes R off ridge down grass to old coach road. Go R down this. **19** After a sharp L turn to bottom it bears R towards pines. **20** Over bridge and along path to clear track. **21** Here sharp R along track. Later bear L up easy pathless grass to col. **22** Over stile near wall corner, and down path. When it becomes vague keep on parallel to fence on L. **23** At post clear path goes half L to gate. Go on through gate for 30 m then turn R down by old wall to road.

37A Shorter walk (11 km, 7 mi, 2500 ft)

Follow walk 37 to wall junction (stage 15). Here turn R by path near wall on your R. When wall turns R keep on to stile in distant wall corner. Here follow stage 22.

After passing the ruins of Tynewydd, an old inn, a short climb gets you back in sight of your starting point. There is an easy short cut that avoids much of the ridge. Once the ridge is reached a mist should not cause problems, as there are fences to follow. There may be a few wet patches e.g. stage 6, 19 (near bridge) and the short cut.

Park (not free) at Cil-cychwyn (634 259). It is reached along a narrow road E from Llanbedr which runs just N of the river at first. Follow signs to Cwm Nantcol. It is ½ mi E of a road junction that is passed after driving nearly 4 mi from Llanbedr.

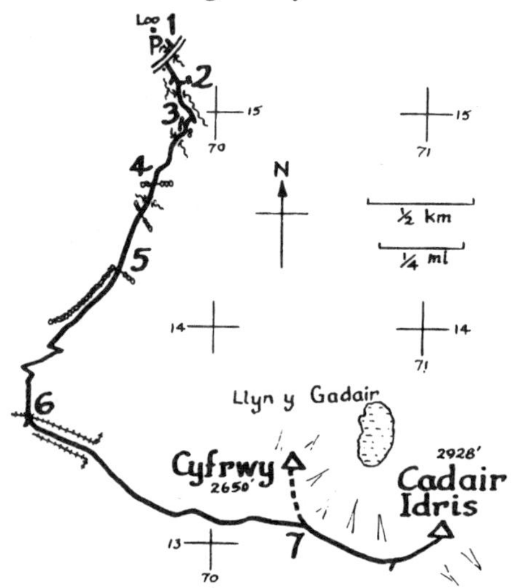

38 CADAIR IDRIS THE EASY WAY

(9 km, 5½ mi, 2400 ft) Map 124, CI

Summary. After a delightful sylvan start there follows a rather featureless section before the final rocky section with superb views. We return the same way as the only alternative, the Foxes path is unpleasantly rough and steep for descent. Paths are mainly dry. There are rough stony sections but the gradients are easy. It is called the Pony Track.

Park at car park (698 153), 4 km (2½ mi) SW of Dolgellau.

1 Leave car park and go R along road 100 m to phone box. Here go L along track. **2** Near farm go on along path over bridge. (Ignore smaller bridge on R.) Path bears L to run by stream. **3** Follow path R between low walls and over bridge. Then it bears L uphill. **4** Go through small gate and SW up field (no path) 100 m to small bridge and on up clear path. **5** Through gate and along by wall, then up zig-zags. **6** At stiles on col go two thirds L along path between fences. (Wettish patch here.) **7** When Llyn y Gadair is seen a detour L to Cyfrwy can be made before the final rise to Cadair Idris.

39 CADAIR IDRIS

(15 km, 9¼ mi, 3100 ft) Map 124, CI

Summary. After a climb through woodland and an open section the long attractive ridge begins by circling Llyn Cau before descending gently (NE) to reach a track back to the road. A parallel track keeps you off the road for quite a distance. Paths

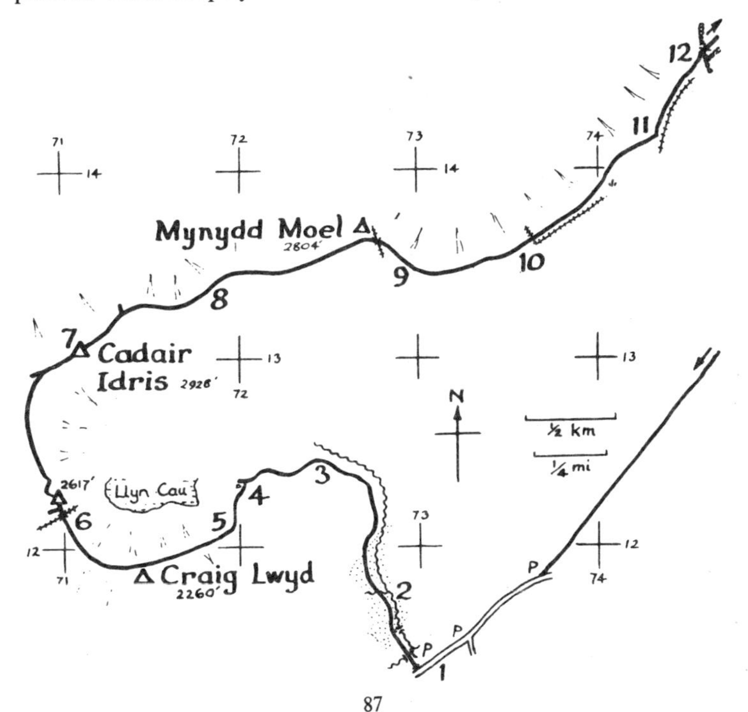

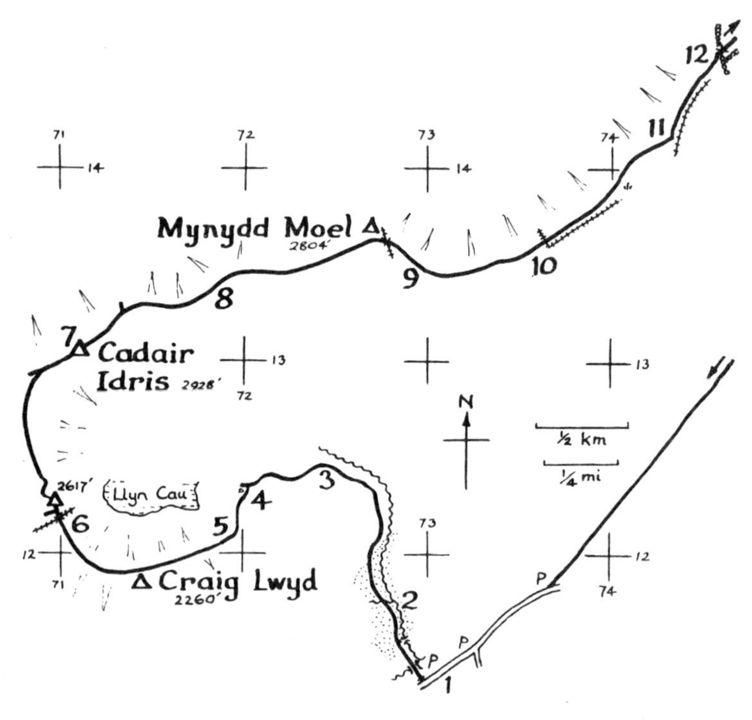

are good — rough in places but not too steep. There may be a few wettish sections well down the ridge. If there is mist beyond the summit it may be better to turn back (or follow walk 39A) as paths in this region are not clear. The alternative descent is shorter, dry and has a pleasant high level section above Tal-y-llyn lake.

Park in car park on the B4405 near its junction with the A487.

1 Go NW through estate gates 300 m SW of road junction (A487/B4405). Cross bridge and go on with stream on your R. **2** After crossing a bouldery stream the path bears away from the stream for a while. **3** At large flattish grassy area path becomes

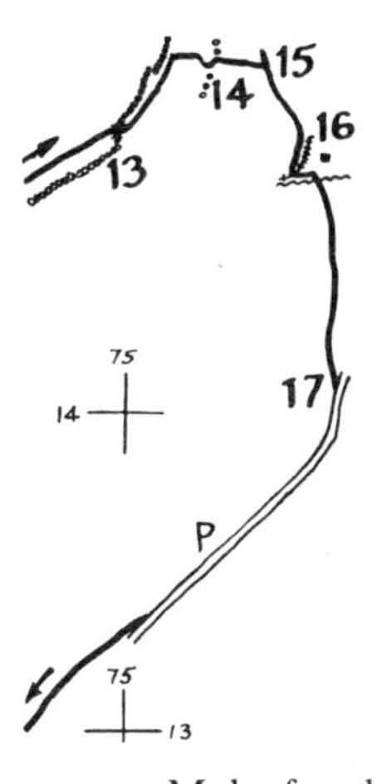

vague. Make for clear stony track along the L side of this area. **4** At large cairn fork L up cairned path. **5** At col go R up ridge (mainly on L of crest). **6** Over stile and on through rocks down path, later bearing R up to Cadair Idris. ● **7** On gently down cairned path. Leave path where it goes L steeply down scree, and carry on over nearly level ground, with steep ground on your L. **8** Where spurs jut out cairns take you a bit further from the edge to avoid bouldery patches. **9** After crossing stile and passing wind shelter path descends more steeply. It crosses the top of a small valley and carries on gently down (E) and up to fence corner. **10** Here go on with fence on your R. At large wet area, path bears L away from fence. **11** It rejoins fence where there are fine views down the steep drop on R of fence. Keep on with fence on your R, soon down a steep section. **12** At wall junction go R over stile and along path near L of wall. **13** Cross wall at stile. Follow wall down to where it turns R for 20 m then L. Go a further 80 m by wall to pass a wet patch and then turn R over dry level grass. (No path.) When ground steepens bear R down to old wall. **14** Here cross wall and go on (E) down grass to track. **15** R along track or in field just R of it. **16** Near stream ignore gate and go by fence (kept on your L) to stile. Then turn L beside stream and soon cross it on stones to reach good path to road. **17** R along road past car park, then fork R down track. On along road when track returns to it.

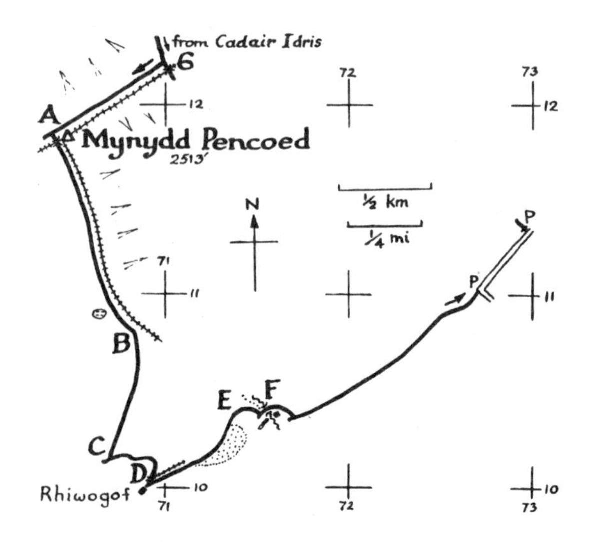

39A Alternative descent (11 km, 7 mi, 3300 ft)
Follow walk 39 to Cadair Idris and turn back to the fence junction at point 6. Here turn R (SW) along ridge with fence on your L. **A** After a slight rise turn L over stile and go down with fence on your L. (Later there is a slight rise near a pool.) **B** When fence is seen to bear L 100 m ahead towards top of a ravine (beyond which are farm buildings), leave fence. Go roughly half R, S then S/SW down pathless easy grass mini-ridge to a track. **C** Turn L along track which winds down to farm (Rhiwogof). **D** Here cross stile and go L along track with hedge/fence on your L. **E** After passing top of wood the track fades. Bear R down edge of trees, then L down the track which is met 50 m before a wall. **F** Cross bridge. Pass L of house and down track to surfaced lane. Go L along lane, then on along road.

Patches of heather survive on vast scree falling from Rhinog Fach to Llyn Hywel. On the right is the ridge path and wall; below them huge rock slabs slant into the Llyn (Walk 37).

INDEX

Note: figures in brackets are the heights of mountains in feet. (Some values are approximate).

Tryfan, as seen from Bristly Ridge.

CHECKLIST OF ITEMS TO TAKE ON WALKS

Rucksack with food (ample in case of delay), drink, first aid, whistle (in case of accident); walking boots, socks; clothes adequate for wet, cold or windy weather; map, compass; watch; money; keys.
(Optional: camera, binoculars, pencil, notebook.)
Check the weather forecast (e.g. phone Llanberis 870120).
In some conditions a torch and survival bag may be needed.

More walking books from Gwasg Carreg Gwalch

Walks on the Llŷn Peninsula